VIOLENCE AGAINST WOMEN

WHAT EVERYONE NEEDS TO KNOW®

JACQUI TRUE

OXFORD
UNIVERSITY PRESS

OXFORD
UNIVERSITY PRESS

Oxford University Press is a department of the University of Oxford. It furthers the University's objective of excellence in research, scholarship, and education by publishing worldwide. Oxford is a registered trade mark of Oxford University Press in the UK and certain other countries.

"What Everyone Needs to Know" is a registered trademark of Oxford University Press.

Published in the United States of America by Oxford University Press 198 Madison Avenue, New York, NY 10016, United States of America.

© Oxford University Press 2021

Library of Congress Control Number: 2020944188
ISBN 978–0–19–937893–7 (pbk.)
ISBN 978–0–19–937894–4 (hbk.)

1 3 5 7 9 8 6 4 2

Paperback printed by Sheridan Books, Inc., United States of America
Hardback printed by Bridgeport National Bindery, Inc., United States of America

VIOLENCE AGAINST WOMEN

WHAT EVERYONE NEEDS TO KNOW®

The patriarchy is a judge
that judges us for being born
and our punishment
is the violence you don't see.
It's femicide.
Impunity for the killer.
It's disappearance.
It's rape.
　　　　　—Colectivo LASTESIS (Chile), *"Un violador en tu*
　　　　　　　　　　camino" ("A rapist in your way")

CONTENTS

7. Culture and VAWG   63

8. VAWG and the Media   73

9. Development, Poverty, and VAWG   81

10. Employment, Precarity, and VAWG   91

PREFACE

Eliminating violence against women and girls (VAWG) globally is one of the major challenges of the 21st century. Since
I first had the idea of writing this book in 2013, awareness of the
problem of violence against women and girls has grown expo-
nentially. This is largely the result of the enormously impactful
#MeToo movement against sexual harassment that began on
social media and diffused around the world (1.7 million tweets
across 85 countries). *Time* magazine made the #MeToo silence
breakers its Person of the Year in 2017, the same year in which
"feminism" was crowned the most searched-for word in the
Merriam-Webster online dictionary. This is hardly surprising
given that 2017 commenced with millions of women and men
joining the pink-hatted Women's March in Washington, DC,
and related marches around the world to denounce sexist rhet-
oric and demand a greater voice for women in political life.

The ensuing years have seen the movement bring about
the removal of many elite men from their positions, including
three members of the US Congress, the mayor of Melbourne,
Australia, and a cabinet minister in the United Kingdom. We
have also seen an avowed harasser elected to the presidency
of the United States and a US Supreme Court justice nom-
inated despite allegations of sexual assault and misconduct.
The proof is in: serial sexual predators are able to achieve professional and political heights. Misogyny, an ideology that

expresses hatred and resentment toward women and thus incites gender-based violence, has re-entered the English lexicon as a result of these violent acts by individuals, be they "incels" (an online community of men who blame women for their lack of sexual intimacy), political leaders, or violent extremist groups ranging from Daesh (ISIS/ISIL) to the alt-right.

Much of the VAWG is of a quantity unknown. This is because it has been historically unrecognized by most societies and experts, and until recently, even by some of its survivors. Regrettably, in some situations violence is so normalized that women and girls come to accept physical, verbal, and sexual abuse as their lot. This lack of individual and societal awareness of VAWG is due in large part to structural gender inequality. This inequality has shaped all of our social, political, and judicial establishments and has meant that, for instance, few institutions have enabled equal access to justice for women and girls. Legislation to prevent and protect against VAWG and to punish its perpetrators is often poorly implemented, is inadequate in its scope and depth, or simply does not exist. Many countries have no consistent definition, baseline data, or systematic documentation of types of violence faced by women and girls. There are few official reports to state agencies, and these barely scratch the surface of actual violence, as indicated by recent UN and World Health Organization (WHO) surveys. There is, moreover, the cruel self-perpetuating nature of VAWG: those experiencing violence may fear that family members, public figures, and institutions such as the police and courts will shame them for speaking out and trivialize the incidents. This consequently stops many women and girls from reporting the violent crimes committed against them. As a result, the cycle of VAWG continues.

Determining whether VAWG is on the increase or is in decline overall is really impossible. That has not stopped some experts from claiming that violence—defined as homicides and casualties from war—is in steady decline globally since the end of World War II. Those claims ignore VAWG as if it were not a proper or recognized type of violence. They fail to acknowledge and methodologically come to terms with the silent and largely unaccounted-for violence perpetrated against women and girls across the centuries. Once we factor in VAWG, including the contemporary incidence of VAWG that we know much more about, we cannot bravely boast that our civilization has been successful in reducing violence—certainly not the violence that is perpetrated against women and girls every day. In fact, if we counted all forms of violence against women and girls listed in the 1993 UN *Declaration on the Elimination of Violence against Women* (DEVAW), total numbers would exceed all the deaths from war in the 20th century.

While we should eschew generalizations about violence and VAWG, in specific contexts we can observe increased VAWG where women and girls are targeted in unique and gender-specific ways compared to men and boys. Two egregious examples readily come to mind. First, since the withdrawal of ISAF troops from Afghanistan in 2014, Afghan women and girls have faced an ongoing legacy of violence. Gendered violence in the form of femicide, honor killings, mutilation, and intimate partner abuse remains widespread throughout the country, and a 2018 UN report lamented that Afghan women still face limited access to justice and significant inequality before the law. Second, as women's presence in political decision-making increases, so too does the rate of violence they encounter. From stalking and physical harassment to more modern practices of online "trolling" and cyberbullying, physical and psychological violence is frequently deployed against politically active women to control, restrict, or inhibit their full and equal political participation.

This book introduces the reader to the problem of violence against women identified by social movements, researchers, and policymakers. It provides key arguments, raw material, macro data, and up-to-date knowledge on VAWG and its intersections with many other issues, as well as the policy, legal, and advocacy frameworks needed to end this violence.

We all have a story to tell about the forms of VAWG that we know of or may have experienced. That is not surprising because even in Victoria, the prosperous state of Australia where I live, intimate partner violence is the leading contributor to death, disability, and illness in women aged 15–44. But while we frequently read or learn about particular experiences or incidents of VAWG, we are often not aware of the full picture. What kinds of violence are we talking about when VAWG is discussed or reported? Who is affected most—that is, who is likely to be the victim and perpetrator? Does VAWG occur in all societies? If so, to what extent? What are the major causes and effects of this violence, and how can we prevent it in our society and other places? Which approaches and solutions show the most promise in reducing VAWG? Are we making any progress in eliminating this violence?

This book addresses the current state of knowledge and research on all of these questions. It surveys our best understanding of the causes and consequences of VAWG in the private home, local community, workplace, public, and transnational realms. In so doing, it traverses multidisciplinary perspectives on the problem, including public health, criminology, sociology, psychology, anthropology, political science, human rights, development studies, gender studies, and international relations/law perspectives, all of which contribute distinct knowledge and insight.

Before going much further, I need to define exactly what VAWG is. This is the focus of chapter 1.

ACKNOWLEDGMENTS

My sincere thanks to Angela Chnapko, my editor at Oxford University Press, for commissioning this book and encouraging me to write it and for bearing with me when it took some time to complete! Thanks also to Alexcee Bechthold for assisting with the publication process and the anonymous reviewers for their suggestions on how to approach the book for a broader readership. I am very grateful to Tamara Ernest for providing research and editing assistance throughout the writing of the book.

Part 1

OVERVIEW AND DEFINITIONS

1

WHAT IS VIOLENCE AGAINST WOMEN AND GIRLS (VAWG)?

What do we mean by VAWG?

"Violence against women and girls" (VAWG) is a catch-all phrase. It includes a wide range of forms of violence. Often when people talk about VAWG in Western societies, they are referring to intimate partner violence or domestic violence in the family or "private" sphere. But VAWG extends beyond these forms and spaces. Women and girls experience abuse and violence within and across multiple sites at home, at work, and in public spaces, and the experience transcends national boundaries, including globalized settings such as international sporting events, national borders during migration, and in special economies or export processing zones with limited legal regulation. Indeed, the very notion of VAWG as a uniquely private-sphere issue is part of the problem in addressing it; that it is merely "private" has served to justify various types of violence against women for centuries. Recall the Napoleonic code, which states that "every man is a king in his own home," and therefore whatever goes on in that home is beyond the purview of the law and the state. We are still living with the legacy of this notion of the private realm and of men's unquestioned power within it.

The most widespread definition of VAWG is that adopted by the United Nations (UN) in 1993 in the General Assembly's

Declaration on the Elimination of Violence against Women (DEVAW). VAWG includes "any act of gender-based violence that results in, or is likely to result in, physical, sexual, or psychological harm or suffering to women, including threats of such acts, coercion or arbitrary deprivation of liberty whether occurring in public or private life." DEVAW characterizes VAWG as the result of "historically unequal power relations between men and women." The UN's *Convention on the Elimination of All Forms of Discrimination against Women* (CEDAW) General Recommendation 19 (1992) is also definitive. CEDAW considers VAWG to be a form of discrimination and a violation of human rights. It succinctly states that VAWG is "violence that affects women and girls disproportionately and/or that is deliberately used to harm women and girls in particular."

In both these international agreements based on a consensus among states, VAWG pertains not only to physical and sexual violence but also to psychological and emotional harm and suffering. Verbal abuse and threats, for instance, count as VAWG. So too does emotional abuse, which includes derogatory comments made in a domineering and disempowering manner about one's worth, personality, body, or emotional state. Often patterns of abuse can be so controlling that the person experiencing them may not be able to recognize that abuse as a form of violence in order to exercise the agency necessary to stop it or leave the situation. This is particularly the case with intimate partner violence, which disproportionately affects young women aged 15–25. In some cases young women may not expect to be treated with respect and dignity if they have grown up in a society or community in which they do not hold a high social status or lack the sense of self-esteem that would be nurtured by families and educational systems that equally value women and girls alongside men and boys.

In 2003 economic violence was added to the UN definition of VAWG. There are egregious cases of economic exploitation of women. For example, the armed group Da'esh in Iraq has trafficked, enslaved, and bartered more than six thousand Yazidi women and girls since 2014, selling them for up to US$165 each.[1] However, economic violence may also be common in an intimate partner or family relationship, in the form of acts that control or monitor the use and distribution of economic resources, and may include forcibly controlling money or other assets, stealing cash, not allowing a woman or girl to take part in any financial decisions, and preventing a woman or girl from gaining employment. This type of VAWG has huge implications not only for women victims but also for the prosperity and well-being of societies generally. Undermining women's economic rights and autonomy through economic violence reduces the available skills and talents that can be harnessed to generate productive capacity in society and limits the overall resources available to meet common goals, not least of which is provision of quality food, shelter, health, and education.

In terms of new understandings of VAWG, online sexual abuse and image-based abuse are currently becoming recognized in international agreements and national legislation. Chapter 8 further explores what constitutes this type of VAWG, as well as how and why it has emerged across societies in a technologically enabled internet age. Similarly, the term "femicide," while not currently featured in international definitions of VAWG, is frequently used to refer to forms of VAWG that result in death. Chapter 3 explores this concept and cases of femicide across the world.

What does "gender-based violence" mean?

Both DEVAW and CEDAW define VAWG as gender-based. But what does it mean to say violence is gender-based? Let's start by defining what is *not* gender-based violence. Violence that affects women and girls as well as men and boys randomly or in a nonspecific or untargeted way is *not* gender-based. For example, a terrorist attack in a tourist hotel that randomly kills civilians including women, men, boys, and girls is not gender-based. However, if that attack specifically targets an area where civilians are disproportionately women and children, or if the attack forcibly uses women and girls as suicide bombers, then it would constitute gender-based violence. To give another example, a mass murder of all the men in a family is not gender-based VAWG. However, that mass murder may be gender-based VAWG if there is an intent to harm or kill based on an ideology of gender or assumptions about gender, such as a belief that only able-bodied men are a threat because they are the ones who bear arms and protect others through the use of force.

There has often been misunderstanding of and pushback against the concept of gender because it challenges the notion that people's identities, roles, and relationships are fixed or determined by nature. The accepted definitions of VAWG, however, understand this violence to be based on gender norms that are readily changeable. They view masculinities and femininities, the roles of women and men (and those who do not identify with binary roles), and the relationships among them to be socially constructed rather than biologically determined.

In 2017 CEDAW updated its definition of VAWG, adopting the term "gender-based violence against women" to make explicit the gendered causes and impacts of the violence. Acknowledging the gender-based nature of VAWG allows us to see the violence as a social—rather than an individual—problem. Gender is understood as a structure or set of power relations that enable violence rather than as a particular individual attribute or role. Given this structure, the CEDAW Committee calls for comprehensive, systematic responses to VAWG instead of responses aimed at individual violent events and vis-à-vis individual perpetrators or victims. The committee considers gender-based VAWG "one of the fundamental social, political and economic means by which the subordinate position of women with respect to men and their stereotyped roles are perpetuated." Violence is employed to reproduce and maintain gender hierarchies; consequently, responses to VAWG must address the larger power structures that contribute to gender-based violence.

Is domestic violence the same thing as family violence, relationship violence, and intimate partner violence?

The term "domestic violence" refers to spousal and nonspousal violence occurring in the family home or household. Although it often denotes intimate partner violence in common usage, the term in fact has a far broader meaning. One concern with domestic violence as a term is that its association with violence in the home, family, or private sphere may unintentionally minimize its threat to individuals, families, communities, and societies more broadly. The word "domestic" is also linked to "domesticate," which encourages us to view the home as an inherently safe place, free from violence. This association again limits our understanding of the seriousness and pervasiveness of VAWG occurring in the home or family. Wherever it occurs, VAWG is violence and is a problem. When people refer to VAWG as "domestic violence," they consciously or subconsciously mask the bigger picture of such violence, which occurs in many different settings, from private to public spheres, in technologically mediated spaces, and within and outside of relationships. To get a sense of the magnitude and scale of "domestic" violence (which continues to be underrecognized relative to its scale), consider that from 2000 to 2012, more women were shot and killed by intimate partners in the United States than the total number of American troops killed during that period in Iraq and Afghanistan combined.[2]

What is the difference between gender-based violence, sexual violence, and the concept of VAWG?

Gender-based violence, sexual violence, and VAWG have distinct but related meanings. This is especially the case because the prominent international definitions now refer to "gender-based violence against women," as mentioned with respect to CEDAW.

Gender-based violence is a crime committed against persons, whether male or female, because of their sex and/or socially constructed gender identity, roles, and relations, that "results in or is likely to result in physical, sexual, psychological, or economic harm or suffering, including threats of such acts, coercion or arbitrary deprivation of liberty." To be considered gender-based violence, attacks on men, boys, women, or girls should be motivated or justified (though not exclusively) by the gender of the individual or group. Examples of this include attacks on or arrests of men, boys, girls, and women for homosexuality; forced nudity or strip searches at checkpoints that may be targeting gender identity and role; sexual harassment of female workers and downgrading of their pay/position as a result; exclusion of trans people or those who identify with a nonbinary gender; and the forcible removal of children from parents that may also target gender and kin relations in the family. In all of these instances, gender may not be the only factor leading to violence against individuals or groups; more often, it intersects with and compounds other factors that lead to violence. Gender and age, for instance, are the critical factors that inform why young women may be seen as easy prey. Equally, the interplay between gender and ethnicity or minority status may motivate violence with the intent of shaming a community in which the honor of girls and women is closely connected to men's identity and roles, as well as group identity and cohesion.

While not always the case, gender-based violence includes and may be manifested as a form of sexual violence. Therefore, sexual violence is considered a subset of gender-based violence. Sexual violence includes an array of crimes beyond rape, including sexual slavery, enforced prostitution, forced pregnancy, forced sterilization, and the imposition of measures intended to prevent births within a group. Sexual violence is listed in the 1998 Rome Statute of the International Criminal Court as violence that constitutes acts of genocide (article 6), crimes against humanity (article 7), and war crimes (article 8). Sometimes sexual harassment at work and sexual abuse of children is included in the concept of sexual violence, which, as a subset of gender-based violence, is in turn related to—though not coterminous with—VAWG.

VAWG addresses violence that either intentionally or disproportionately affects women and girls, whereas gender-based violence exploits gender inequalities, differences, and hierarchies, be they among women, girls, men, boys, or people who do not identify with binary gender. As previously discussed, VAWG consists of different *types of violence* (physical, sexual, psychological, emotional, and economic) as well as the *forms* it takes (intimate partner violence, rape, acid burning, forced marriage, trafficking, and so on). In some parts of the world "VAWG" is the preferred term because of its legal basis and incorporation of gender-based VAWG. However, it does not typically consider gender-based violence against men and boys. That is not to say, however, that gender-based violence does not affect men and boys.

Do men and boys experience gender-based violence?

Yes, they do. Gender-based violence incorporates crimes committed against all sexes and gender identities, which includes men and boys. A classic case of gender-based violence is the practice of *bacha bazi* in Afghanistan, in which impoverished boys or young men are trafficked and sold to older men for use as dancers and sexual playthings. Based on the definition of gender-based violence in this book, these boys experience gender-based violence systematically; their abuse is so normalized that some consider it a part of Afghan culture, with Afghan men openly flaunting their *bacha bazi* boys and the authorities (including government officials) largely dismissing calls to investigate or end the practice.[3] Far from being a cultural nuance, *bacha bazi* is a harmful traditional practice that is increasingly being exposed by international organizations (the UN, Human Rights Watch, and the Afghanistan Independent Human Rights Commission, among others) as a form of violence and abuse of power. The male experience of gender-based violence has also come to light in conflict scenarios in Bosnia, Uganda, Iraq, and Sudan, where men and boys have faced homosexualization, feminization, genital harm, and sex-selective killing as a means to humiliate, emasculate, and divest them of their power and masculine identities. Of course in many circumstances of male gender-based violence, gender stereotypes and concepts around masculinity may prevent men from disclosing the gender-based violence perpetrated against them, leading to incomplete data on its scope and prevalence.[4]

This book focuses on gender-based VAWG. However, gender-based violence perpetrated against men and boys and people of non-binary gender is mentioned throughout because gender-based violence against men and boys is part of the very same problem and a product of the very same gender structure of power relations that affects women and girls, with similar, if not the same, root causes and solutions.

2

HISTORICAL STRUGGLE

How did VAWG first gain recognition?

Violence against women and girls—from marital rape and wife battering to sexual abuse and harassment—has largely been hidden in recorded history, though the problem extends back well beyond our mothers' and grandmothers' generations. Similarly, the struggle against this violence has also always formed part of our history, albeit consisting mostly of undocumented and untold stories.

Testifying to its widespread acceptance and normalization, only relatively recently has VAWG been identified as a problem, let alone one worthy of study. Most societies have historically been shaped by religious doctrines that centralized male authority within all types of institutions, be they faith based, state, civil society, or family. Religious scriptures have been—and in some cases still are—interpreted by male leaders, who highlight writings that depict women as inherently inferior or subservient to men. Indeed, the belief that violence within the home is a private matter has roots in past legal sanctions of male dominance within the family and under God. In Roman law, for instance, husbands and fathers had the right to "chastise" wives and children physically; in English common law, men were allowed to beat their wives with a stick; and in some versions of sharia law, such violence by male family members is also sanctioned. This connection between male dominance and violence against women went largely unnoticed and unstudied until advocates for women's rights began to enter the academy in greater numbers, establishing the studies of women and gender relations as legitimate subjects for education and research in their own right.

In the 1970s established power relations began to be questioned and challenged as people sought alternatives to traditional gender roles. The women's liberation movement took off alongside the civil rights and environmental social movements, re-examining status quo gender and race relations in societies. Men's violence against women became a key issue around which women's groups mobilized. In 1975 Susan Brownmiller published *Against Our Will*, challenging male rape. Divorce rates grew in the 1970s, in part due to women walking out of violent relationships. Women's consciousness-raising (in which women in a group shared common experiences of sex discrimination and violence) played a part in this trend, as did the practical availability of battered women's shelters and other services provided by communities and governments that offered protection, alternative housing, and financial support.

The contrast between the public treatment of women today and that of 50 years ago is stark in many respects. An example is the Profumo affair in the United Kingdom in 1963, in which powerful, elite men mixed with young working-class women in orchestrated recreational settings. One such relationship that came into public view was between John Profumo, secretary of state for war, and Christine Keeler, a 19-year-old aspiring model. Through their relationship and many others, sex—what we might later see as a type of violence based on the exploitation of young women—became a visible part of high politics. The published version of the commissioned inquiry into the affair became a best seller, boasting 100,000 sales within a few days of publication. However, the public fascination was with a sex scandal and Cold War paranoia: sex rather than violence, the security of the state rather than the security of women, and the abuse of power rather than the abuse of power over women. The stigma of the Profumo affair attached to Christine Keeler made it difficult for her to find work for decades afterward, while the reputation of the British Conservative Party was not so marred.[1]

Fast-forward to the late 1990s and the threatened impeachment of US president Bill Clinton. His affair with Monica Lewinsky was as fascinating to the public as the Profumo affair had been in 1960s Britain. However, by this stage the frame had begun to alter; Monica Lewinsky's story was aired on national television in the United States. Her experience of abuse of power by a male authority was not the main story (the president's marital infidelity and pending impeachment were), but in this saga a young woman's voice was taken marginally more seriously than in the case of Christine Keeler, although Lewinsky was the subject of mockery in the US press at the time for her disclosures. Looking further ahead to today's #MeToo movement, we now place women at the center of news stories. The public "outing" of Jeffrey Epstein suggests a sea change in the public acceptance of the involvement of very elite men in deliberate sexual exploitation and violence against women, in this case the trafficking of young women. While Epstein got away with this for a number of years even after first being exposed, the case has been treated with seriousness, elite men (such as Prince Andrew of the United Kingdom) have had power and prestige taken away, and the women victims have a prominent voice in the media accounts.

In naming their perpetrators and speaking out about the violence they have experienced, women have redefined themselves from victims to agents in combating VAWG. Power is shifting. Until it does, we cannot recognize VAWG. Change happens, slower than we would like; this is the stuff of the longue durée.

How central was the women's movement to the recognition of VAWG?

The fight against violence against women was central to second wave feminism in the late 1960s and 1970s, especially among women's liberation groups that emerged in the United States, Europe, and other Western democracies. Women involved in the US civil rights, antiwar, and black liberation movements against racial oppression and state-sanctioned violence came to question their own (often subordinate) positions in these movements vis-à-vis men, as well as their common experiences of men's violence. Women's movements began to spread across the world, raising issues of women's lack of control over their bodies, sexuality and sexual relationships, and reproductive choices: when, where, and whether or not to have children. The Boston Women's Collective's *Our Bodies, Ourselves* (1971), which provided frank discussion on women's health issues, became a worldwide best seller. As the contraceptive pill allowed some women a measure of autonomy, women's movements now sought to mobilize around further control of their bodies, families, and lives.

These movements also discussed the unequal gender divisions of labor, which held women primarily responsible for unpaid (and therefore often unrecognized) care work. Care work includes giving birth to and raising children; providing sexual, emotional, and affective services in the household; maintaining family and intimate relationships; producing goods and services in the home; carrying out voluntary work to meet community needs; and keeping and passing on cultural traditions to the next generation. In view of this, radical and socialist feminist groups demanded an egalitarian restructuring of male/female relationships and society by claiming that "the personal is political": what happens in relations between women and men and in the so-called privacy of the home is deeply political and a form of power. As feminist theorist Susan Moller Okin succinctly put it, many women were "one man's affection away from poverty"; without an independent income or alternative housing and support for themselves and their children, there was little opportunity to escape the violence of an abusive husband or partner.

Fundamentally, women's movements brought women closer to a collective reckoning about the hidden violence they faced. Women came to realize that their experiences of violence were not unique and shameful but shared and problematic. Together they broke the silence about men's power over women, including men's violence against women and girls. They created an environment in which women could speak about the abuse and violence inflicted on them without self-blame. Women thinkers and leaders showed how the private power of men shaped public power and societal institutions, such as the legal justice system, systems of government, and religious institutions, none of which had recognized or addressed VAWG.

Once VAWG was recognized within women's movements, diverse groups began working on strategies for change that emphasized providing services responsive to women survivors, changing the law to prosecute VAWG, and introducing new policies to prevent this violence and realize gender justice. The "shelter movement" for women survivors of domestic or intimate partner violence, as well as antirape and antipornography groups, emerged in the 1970s. In the United States this gave way to the emergence of battered women's coalitions, which changed the conventional image of abused women by recognizing them as victimized and blameless rather than passive, dependent, and deviant. In short, they created a new image of abused women. For instance, an early model in the United States, the Duluth Domestic Abuse Intervention Project, aimed to develop women's self-organizing capacities and viewed the state as a male or masculine leader. Similarly, in the United Kingdom, activist and writer Sheila Rowbotham identified women's shelters as a "prefigurative form" for a more gender-just state and society.[2] The Duluth project and similar endeavors around the world defended women's individual rights and protections, reflecting the norms of the liberal state.

By the late 1970s the state had begun to listen to the call of women's movements and to fund battered women's shelters. While this recognition gave legitimacy to the VAWG movement, it undermined the feminist philosophy and self-organizing strategy underpinning the movement. By the 1980s women's grassroots activism that focused on empowering women was transformed into social service agencies serving clients. Consequently, feminist political analysis of violence as linked to the power relations of men over women was diffused and (arguably) weakened; the liberating discourses challenging patriarchy and female dependency that had shaped the women's movement morphed into discourses on crime control and punishment of individual perpetrators. We now tend to focus on arresting, prosecuting, and punishing perpetrators of domestic and family violence rather than on other measures to stop this violence that address the power inequalities behind why it happens in the first place. Leigh Goodmark, for instance, shows how criminalization of domestic violence as the main approach to violence prevention coincides with mass incarceration in the United States, with rates of imprisonment increasing fivefold during the anti–domestic violence movement.[3]

Mass action on VAWG was crucial early on in the VAWG movement and is equally important today. For example, the 1977 Take Back the Night (TBTN) or Reclaim the Night campaign in the United Kingdom began an annual tradition of women in London, Manchester, and Leeds walking the streets as a collective to combat rape and sexual violence against women, often with key demands directed at the state. In the Netherlands and West Germany, women dressed as witches and marched with music and torches; on US university campuses, activists hung life-sized silhouettes representing women who had been killed by men's violence. That tradition rapidly spread and globalized; in 2011 it morphed into the "SlutWalk"

(2011–present), an international movement to protest the culture of blaming and shaming victims of sexual violence. The movement's slogan—"wherever we go, whatever we wear, yes means yes and no means no"—was renewed in a new generation of activism.[4]

Ultimately, the TBTN movement made and continues to make visible women's anger about sexual violence. By using women's experiences to highlight the rape culture that pervades societies, the movement has supported the work and outreach of rape crisis centers and battered women's shelters. However, hindsight has revealed some deficits; a 1984 critique by Valerie Amos and Pratibha Parmar claimed that TBTN actually worsened conditions in communities of color. They charged US marches through black inner-city areas with fueling vigilante groups patrolling the streets to "protect" innocent white women by beating up black men.[5] Nowadays the movement has enacted changes to incorporate concerns from communities of color, including black and indigenous women. The TBTN/Reclaim the Night events take place at different times throughout the world, including in late April in the United States, in the last week of October in Australia (to conclude Sexual Violence Awareness Month), and in late November in the United Kingdom. These events complement the 16 Days of Activism against Gender-Based Violence campaign, which runs from November 25 (International Day for the Elimination of VAW) to December 10 (International Human Rights Day). Indeed, the origin of this campaign is credited to Latin American and Caribbean feminist activists, who in 1981 chose November 25 as the date to commemorate the murder of three Dominican political activists by state security forces in the 1960s.[6] The date received official United Nations (UN) status in 1999.

How did VAWG gain recognition globally? What has been the role of the UN in promoting awareness of VAWG?

Global recognition of VAWG has occurred through both the transnational diffusion of women's movements and advocacy based on international human rights. Initially, distinct campaigns in different global regions protested diverse types of violence: in the United States and Europe it was rape and domestic violence; in Africa, female genital mutilation; in India and Bangladesh, dowry death; in East Asia and Southeast Asia, wartime comfort women, sex tourism, and exploitation of female migrant workers; and in Latin America, state violence against women, including the torture and rape of political prisoners. In the 1980s and 1990s these campaigns converged in a political space forged by women's movements and broadcast by the UN. Activists began to see a basic common denominator in their activism—a belief in the importance of women's bodily integrity—enabling them to establish solidarity in antiviolence movements across different nationalities and cultures.

At much the same time, the UN Decade for Women (1975–1985) and UN World Conferences on Women (Mexico City in 1975, Copenhagen in 1980, Nairobi in 1985, and Beijing in 1995) catalyzed networks of women's movements and built momentum for states to address the global injustices faced by women and girls. In particular, Nairobi was the first conference to make substantial recommendations on the issue of violence against women, including the official formation of the International Network against Violence against Women (INAVAW).

Just as important as attendance was the language adopted at these global events. With each new world conference and campaign, the language of gender injustice became more institutionalized, global minded, and persuasive. In statements, various anti-VAWG groups and campaigns adopted similar wording, text, and arguments to advocate for change on behalf of women in vastly different social, political, and cultural contexts. As the UN's *Declaration on the Elimination of Violence against Women* (DEVAW) of 1993 and Beijing Platform for Action of 1995 were quoted and requoted, women's rights activists hoped that states would begin to conform to these norms in their policies and practices.

Under the ambit of the UN, the framing of VAWG began to shift from antidiscrimination to a more human rights–based approach. This required due diligence on the part of states to create the conditions under which rights—for instance, the right to bodily integrity—could be enjoyed by all. This framework was reinforced in the slogan of the 1995 UN Beijing Women's Conference, at which then-US first lady Hillary Clinton famously stated that "women's rights are human rights." This reconceptualization broadened human rights organizations and enabled them to better include women—as half of humanity and often having distinct needs—in their vision of rights violations.

In a similar vein, agreement was reached at the UN World Conference on Human Rights (Vienna, 1993) that integrating women's concerns into the human rights agenda and recognizing gender-based violence against women as a human rights violation were crucial to advancing the international protection of human rights. In many respects the human rights methodology lent itself to this goal because it aimed to promote change through the reporting of facts, including the incidence of violence. Specifically, this methodology required nongovernmental organizations (NGOs) to document violence and abuse, demonstrate state accountability for these abuses under international law, and develop mechanisms for exposing them nationally and internationally. At the same time, women's movements across the globe acknowledged that the violation of women's right to bodily integrity was an issue that crossed national, class, racial, age, sexuality, and ethnic lines. By the 1995 UN World Women's Conference, VAWG was given central prominence, and women's rights activists had developed sophisticated lobbying strategies to influence the final Beijing

Platform for Action, which was adopted by all states present. At Beijing, women's rights activists argued that gender inequality enables VAWG and, moreover, that the success of any effort to eradicate this violence would depend on local and national action frameworks. This global attention on VAWG during the Beijing conference placed pressure on national governments and created the necessary political momentum for women to advocate for change.

What were the debates in women's movements in the 1980s and 1990s about combining different kinds of injustice and oppression in a global concept of VAWG?

Alongside the UN Decade for Women, the second UN Development Decade (1971–1980) highlighted the economic inequality faced by women around the world, in part due to global restructuring and development. Specifically, women in the Global South, through organizations such as Development Alternatives for Women in a New Era (DAWN), called for changes in structural economic conditions, including equal property and inheritance rights, access to credit for rural women, and decent work opportunities for rural women. Whereas women's rights activism in Western countries was focused on ending discrimination and increasing access to political institutions, women's activism in the South highlighted colonial legacies, social justice, and the negative effects of international financial frameworks and economic development policies. For example, structural adjustment policies promoted by the International Monetary Fund in loan recipient developing countries starting in the 1980s forced them to reduce spending on health and education and incentivize cash-cropping, with disproportionate impacts on the livelihoods of women farmers and women in households, who were responsible for the well-being of children, the elderly, and other family members. The latter in particular shaped women's vulnerability to VAWG in the Global South; as such, any analysis of the root causes of this violence needed to address the structural violence of poverty and economic inequality.

Similarly, there was a need to address violence in the family as part of the overall picture of VAWG. Following the Beijing conference in 1995, the creation of the UN Special Rapporteur on Violence Against Women allowed for a more nuanced and comprehensive investigation of VAWG across varied contexts, shifting from a public focus (violence by the state) to incorporate private experiences (violence by individuals within the home or community). The first Special Rapporteur, Sri Lankan lawyer Radhika Coomaraswamy, identified that the family was the main site of violence against women and argued that the justification of VAWG within negative cultures and traditions must be eliminated. In 1995 traditional practices harmful toward women were explicitly identified by the Special Rapporteur, who called for greater education and women's empowerment to reduce the incidence of this form of violence, particularly in developing countries.

3

MAPPING VAWG GLOBALLY

Is VAWG a global epidemic?

Violence against women and girls is a global epidemic. It has been described as the most prevalent yet least recognized human rights violation, widespread across all countries in both urban and rural areas. On average, 35 percent of women and girls will experience one violent incident in their lives after the age of 16 years; this overall international victimization rate is based on a conservative definition of physical violence, which is believed to underestimate VAWG.

The most pervasive type of VAWG is abuse by intimate male partners. With this specific type of VAWG, there is significant variation in prevalence and form across countries and across groups, suggesting that intimate partner violence is not inevitable but rather can be reduced and prevented. A recent review of 50 population-based studies carried out in 36 countries indicated that between 10 and 60 percent of women who have ever been married or partnered have experienced at least one incident of physical violence from a current or former intimate partner.[1] The World Health Organization's (WHO) 2005 multicountry study found that the form of intimate partner violence varied culturally; for instance, the proportion of women who had suffered physical violence by a male partner ranged from 13 percent in Japan to 61 percent in provincial Peru, while just 6 percent of women and girls reported experiencing sexual violence in urban Serbia and Montenegro, compared to 59 percent of women and girls in Ethiopia. Importantly, the data used by WHO was gained from surveying over 24,000 women across 15 locations in 10 countries, representing diverse geographic and cultural settings.

More broadly, sexual coercion as a form of sexual violence, in which a woman or girl lacks choice and faces severe physical or social consequences if she resists sexual advances, is definitive of "being female" for many women and girls. With respect to sexual violence, most studies report that the prevalence of this abuse among girls is significantly higher than among boys—at least 1.5 to 3 times higher. Furthermore, studies consistently show that the vast majority of perpetrators are male and are known to their victims, regardless of their sex. This gendered pattern of sexual coercion is global, a feature of every society and country. Countries vary most in the extent of non-intimate-partner VAWG, which includes sexual violence. The International Violence against Women Survey (IVAWS) found that between 20 and 60 percent of women and girls had reported at least one incident of physical or sexual violence since they were 16 years of age. Importantly, while VAWG has always existed, over time new global trends in the type of violence perpetrated against women and girls have emerged, such as acid attacks and the recognition of female genital mutilation/cutting as a type of VAWG.

Acid attacks—throwing acid or other corrosive chemical substances on a victim—are a relatively new type of VAWG occurring globally, but they are particularly common in South Asia and the Middle East and overwhelmingly target women and girls. Action is being taken to address this popular form of VAWG: in 2002, Bangladesh strengthened criminal laws regarding acid attacks to improve and heighten criminal procedures and penalties, as well as to decrease the availability of acid. As a result, acid attacks have dropped 15 to 20 percent annually. Likewise, in 2013 India amended its penal code to legislate against acid attacks and has attempted to regulate the sale of acid. In Cambodia, too, the government has recently drafted new laws to address acid violence, in particular seeking to regulate the sale of acid, as well as introducing harsh punishment for perpetrators of acid violence. That being said, loopholes in legislation have meant that a culture of impunity continues to exist with regard to acid attacks in several countries.

Female genital mutilation/cutting (FGM/C) is a contentious type of VAWG, only recognized as violence in DEVAW. A traditional practice usually affecting girls under the age of 14, FGM/C encompasses all procedures that involve injury to external female genitalia and/or female genital organs. Once widespread due to its cultural significance, the practice has declined greatly due to laws and societal campaigns seeking to challenge its use. Ngianga-Bakwin Kandala and her colleagues studied 210,000 children in 29 countries and found the steepest rate of decline was in East Africa, where FGM/C rates fell from 71.4 percent in 1995 to just 8 percent in 2016.[2]

Finally, there has been a rise in new types of VAWG linked to the use of technology, including online abuse; stalking on/offline; image-based abuse (which involves the dissemination of compromising sexualized images and child pornography); and the phenomenon of "sexting," in which images are shared via texts and other messaging services and e-platforms. Chapter 8 discusses these types of VAWG in greater depth with respect to the relationship between VAWG and global media.

Which groups of women and girls are most affected by VAWG?

There is also great variation in the extent of VAWG across different groups within countries with respect to age, ethnicity, socioeconomic status, immigrant status, indigeneity, sexuality, disability, and rural/urban dwelling. According to Australia's National Research Organization for Women's Safety (ANROWS), for instance, indigenous females are 5 times more likely to be victims of homicide than nonindigenous females and 35 times as likely to be hospitalized due to family-violence-related assaults. We also know that younger women are at significantly higher risk of violence—especially sexual violence—than older women; the US Rape, Abuse & Incest National Network (RAINN) reports that women aged 65 and older are 92 percent less likely than those aged 12–24 to be victims of rape or sexual assault, and 83 percent less likely than women aged 25–49. Women living in rural areas experience the greatest prevalence of violence, although evidence from UN-Habitat suggests that while VAWG by male partners is higher in rural than in urban areas, violence by nonpartners is higher in urban areas, especially in informal settlements with poor access to lighting, sanitation, and transport.[3]

Across the world, women and girls with a disability or long-term health condition face a higher risk of violence. According to the UN Trust Fund (2017), disabled women and girls suffer up to three times greater risk of rape, are twice as likely to experience domestic violence, and are more likely to suffer abuse over a longer period of time and with more harmful injuries than women without disabilities. The risk to disabled women and girls is acutely global, with similar findings in Latin America by Inter-American Development Bank (2019) and throughout several central African countries by Humanity & Inclusion (2018).[4] These reports suggest that increased isolation, dependence on an abusive partner, and a lack of adequate resources for reporting are some of the key factors that contribute to the increased rate of violence faced by disabled women and girls.

Migrant women also experience a greater rate of violence. As more and more women migrate independently (a trend known as the feminization of migration), they face increased vulnerability and exposure to different kinds of gender-based risks, including abuse by fellow migrants, extortion, trafficking and organized migration for marriage, and violence perpetrated by migration agents and security forces. Once settled, migrant women remain key targets of economic violence in the form of forced labor, exploitation, withholding of pay, under- or non-payment, and discrimination in the workplace. Immigration status insecurity and insufficient legal protections for migrant workers further exacerbate their risk.

Overall, we can see that women with less power, fewer social and economic rights, and less access to resources are more likely to experience vulnerability to violence. Furthermore, women's experience of violence is different depending on the intersectionality of their identities and positionality. Women who face one or more barriers due to race/ethnicity, sexuality, nationality, disability, and so on are ultimately more disadvantaged; when several of these axes of identity overlap, their risk of VAWG is exacerbated.

What national and international data and statistics on VAWG are available?

Several cross-sectional surveys and studies have already been mentioned. Of particular note are the International Violence Against Women Surveys (IVAWS) and the longitudinal Demographic and Health Surveys (DHS), which are standardized, population-based household surveys conducted across select countries to collect data on intimate partner violence and sexual violence. The DHS are often commissioned by donor agencies in developing countries where there is less infrastructure to support violence prevention. There are also discrete national surveys—such as the US National Survey conducted by the Centers for Disease Control (CDC)—that explore a range of self-reported types of violence. Furthermore, some generic household or individual surveys—for instance, the CDC-supported International Reproductive Health Surveys (IRHS)—increasingly contain ancillary questions on VAWG as part of a broader investigation into a range of justice, crime, and health issues. While based on self-reporting, these surveys ask very specific questions to generate an overall estimate of the prevalence of VAWG. For physical violence, the questions women and girls are asked include whether a current or former partner has ever slapped her; thrown something at her that could hurt her; pushed or shoved her; hit her with a fist or something else that could hurt; kicked her, dragged her, or beaten her up; choked or burned her on purpose; or threatened her with or actually used a gun, knife, or other weapon against her. Framing the questions in this manner ensures that women who may not see certain behaviors as violent (or see some behaviors as violent but not others) are still counted in the survey.

Producing reliable comparative data across countries to identify and monitor the patterns of VAWG is extremely difficult. Different definitions and measurements of VAWG in different surveys mean that meaningful comparisons between studies and reliable estimates of VAWG across contexts cannot be made. Consequently, there is great reliance on large multicountry studies conducted by single or umbrella organizations that can produce consistent data points on the experience of VAWG across several categories. Indeed, the WHO study previously mentioned is one of the few that used the same methodology across sites, thereby enabling comparison of VAWG prevalence rates.

How valid are these data and trends on VAWG given the problem of nonreporting?

Many factors may obstruct reporting about VAWG. A frequently observed pattern in VAWG data is the "tip of the iceberg" phenomenon, in which there is a high prevalence rate but low level of reporting. However, it is a common misconception to equate greater reporting of VAWG with greater VAWG. Increased reporting among certain groups and in certain areas of a country or region may not reflect the actual scale, severity, or diversity of the types of violence or even the location of the violence, since survivors may choose to report outside their local area. Rather, increased reporting of VAWG merely indicates better reporting institutions and referral pathways for victims. Consequently, where there exist specific, tailored institutions to receive reports on VAWG, such as police stations or women police units, as in Brazil or the Philippines, we would expect to see more reports of VAWG. That being said, there are often other intervening factors, such as the stigma associated with being a victim of violence; the shame that victims may experience in their families and communities; and the existence of alternative dispute resolution mechanisms in the family, community, or religious institutions that hamper data gathering on the true incidence of violence.

Whom do women turn to, and whom do they tell about, the violence in their lives? While some women are able to leave home and others can endure the violence, the shocking answer in a significant number of cases is that they have nobody. In response to this, several countries have strengthened their reporting institutions in recent years to ensure greater access to justice. In India, a 2018 study recorded a 22 percent increase in reports of crimes against women in cities with all-women police units, drawing the conclusion that women felt more comfortable reporting crimes perpetrated against them when in the presence of female officers.[5] Increased reporting can also arise away from law enforcement, through access to community legal centers, family planning units, and women's shelters. In Bosnia and Herzegovina, for instance, UN Women reported that extended paralegal services targeting victims of domestic violence in the marginalized Roma communities have resulted in a 50 percent increase in requests for help; similarly, in North Macedonia, civil society organizations providing free legal aid services to women and girls recorded a 60 percent increase in the number of survivors seeking justice.[6]

What are the most dangerous places and spaces to be a woman or girl?

Not surprisingly, the most dangerous places for women and girls are countries without comprehensive laws on VAWG and responsive justice institutions. In 2011, TrustLaw Women conducted a poll asking 213 global gender discrimination and equality experts to rank the most dangerous countries in the world. The survey included aid professionals, health workers, academics, policymakers, journalists, and development specialists. They were interviewed about the most dangerous countries for women and girls in terms of healthcare; access to economic resources; sexual and nonsexual abuse; traditional harmful practices; and human trafficking, including domestic servitude, forced labor, sexual slavery, and forced marriage. The results ranked Afghanistan as the most dangerous country for women and girls, followed by the Democratic Republic of Congo (DRC), Pakistan, India, and Somalia. Afghanistan was rated the most dangerous country for health, economic resources, and nonsexual violence; the DRC for sexual violence; Pakistan for traditional practices; and India for human trafficking. In related surveys, Bogota, Colombia, was ranked the most unsafe transport system for women among the world's 15 largest capital cities, and India the most unsafe G20 country for women.[7]

In 2018 a similar survey asked which five countries were most dangerous for women across the same six areas, using similar experts.[8] The findings revealed that the ranking order had changed: India was now named the world's most dangerous for women overall, with extremely high levels of violence against women. This was exemplified in 2013 when a 23-year-old student on a bus in Delhi was raped and murdered, sparking national and international outrage and a government inquiry to tackle the issue. Overall, India ranked the most dangerous on three issues: the risks women face from sexual violence and harassment; harmful traditional practices;

and human trafficking, including forced labor, sex slavery, and domestic servitude (note that in the previous survey, India was only the worst-ranked with respect to trafficking). We might interpret these results for India in particular as stemming from increased knowledge of VAWG subsequent to the Delhi rape, with more media and researchers paying attention to trends and data in the country. Beyond this, Afghanistan and Syria ranked second and third on the list, both having endured years of conflict that have resulted in poor access to healthcare and economic resources for women, as well as high levels of non-sexual violence and domestic abuse.

Interestingly, the United States ranked third alongside Syria with regard to the risk of sexual abuse faced by women, and sat at 10th place overall—the only Western country in the top 10. This survey result somewhat reflects higher reporting in Western, developed countries and is also perhaps indicative of a new openness to reporting on sexual harassment and abuse in the United States, as shown by the very public #MeToo movement and its social media following.

We can also answer the question about the most dangerous places for women and girls with respect to spaces within cities, villages, and rural areas. Women's access to certain public and private spaces is regulated according to their dress, behavior, and/or social interactions. Marketplaces, cafes, sporting clubs, and other seemingly public spaces may be prohibited for women in some societies. When women enter spaces where their presence is not socially sanctioned, they may be more vulnerable to violence, given the lack of social mores inhibiting men's VAWG in these spaces. In response to these trends, creating safe cities for women has become an international movement, particularly with the establishment of UN-Habitat's Safe Cities Free of VAWG Initiative. This global program, which runs in Ecuador, Egypt, India, Papua New Guinea, and Rwanda, aims to evaluate approaches to respond to and prevent sexual harassment and sexual violence against women and girls in public spaces.

Even the public spaces that women occupy can pose a risk. For instance, sexual harassment perpetrated on public transport is especially common in large cities of rising, middle-income countries, such as New Delhi, Cairo, Colombo, Mexico City, and Jakarta. When transport connections are poorly lit and isolated, and/or bus and train carriages are overcrowded, and where gender relations are rapidly changing in the context of urbanization, women's ability to move safely around cities is severely constrained. Violence against women and girls is also more likely to occur in public spaces around toilets, schools, and bars, and in secluded areas like narrow lanes and open fields. Public toilets that are located away from people's dwellings, such as in refugee and displacement camps or in rural areas, pose an even greater risk of violence, especially at night. That being said, contrary to most assumptions about safety, it is in fact private spaces such as the family home (rather than public ones) that women and girls generally face the highest risk of violence.

4

VAWG AND GENDER DISCRIMINATION, INEQUALITY, AND POWER

Is gender discrimination a form of VAWG?

Discriminatory gender norms may be reflected in laws, such as criminal laws that prohibit violent acts occurring in the public realm but not in the home, and civil laws that do not allow women to pass on their citizenship to their children (assuming a man's or father's citizenship is definitive). Norms that discriminate based on gender may also be embedded in government policies that deport victims of sex trafficking or domestic violence without providing safe passage or asylum, or employment policies that provide leave for sports injuries but not for injuries from domestic violence. While not constituting violence in themselves, these types of gender discriminatory practices are societal conditions that contribute to power imbalances and a culture of impunity for certain types of violence against women, thereby increasing the likelihood of its occurrence.

The UN's CEDAW (1979), signed and ratified by 189 states, considers that violence against women is a form of gender discrimination that negatively impacts women globally: "Gender-based violence is a form of discrimination that seriously inhibits women's ability to enjoy rights and freedoms on a basis of equality with men." CEDAW, which previously focused on ending discrimination against women in political, economic, social, cultural, and civil arenas without any reference to VAWG, chose to revise its agenda to adopt General Recommendation 19 on violence against women in 1992. In General Recommendation 19, CEDAW defines discrimination against women to include gender-based violence, that is, "violence that is directed against a woman because she is a woman or that affects women disproportionately" (as discussed in chapter 1). In Recommendation 28, a 2010 revision, CEDAW acknowledges that discrimination against women including violence against women is compounded by intersecting forms of discrimination based on age, race, ethnicity, immigrant status, disability, sexuality, and so on. In General Recommendation 35, the Convention also addresses the distinct violence affecting women and girls arising from gender-based discrimination in conflict situations.

The connection between gender discrimination and VAWG is explicitly acknowledged in the 2030 sustainable development goals (SDGs), which promise, upon achievement, to make the world more peaceful as well as more environmentally and economically secure. Goal 5 sets out to end all forms of discrimination against women and girls everywhere and to eliminate all forms of violence against women and girls and all harmful practices, including child and forced marriage and FMG/C. There is mounting evidence that women and girls cannot fully participate in social, political, and economic life if they continue to face pervasive violence in the home, in the public sphere, and at work. Furthermore, women and girls can function more freely in society and in the business world when not faced by the threat of violence, as discussed later in this book with respect to the significant societal, economic, and environmental impacts of VAWG.

Do gender discrimination and VAWG usually co-occur?

Discriminatory gender norms, such as those that assume men's status/behavior to be the norm or that perpetuate bias in laws and policies, serve as the root causes of violence. This is because these norms promote the acceptance and spread of violence by encouraging aggressive and violent masculinities and relatively silent femininities. Thus, gender discrimination in a society, especially where it is systemic, frequently co-occurs with a high prevalence of reported VAWG.

We can see the strength of the relationship between gender discrimination and VAWG if we compare the Organisation for Economic Co-operation and Development's (OECD) Social Institutions and Gender Index (SIGI), which measures the extent of gender discrimination from very low to very high, with the WHO Demographic and Health Surveys, which measure two types of VAWG: physical intimate partner violence and sexual violence. The OECD SIGI is the best available indicator for gender discrimination by country, including 180 countries in 2019. It provides a composite measure of discrimination against women in social institutions, as reflected in discriminatory societal practices and legal norms that produce inequalities between women and men. The SIGI captures gender discrimination, the factors contributing to it, and the various ways in which discrimination manifests in five subindexes: restricted physical integrity, discriminatory family codes, son-bias (which is related to female infanticide and technologies to prevent the birth of females), restricted civil liberties, and restricted resources and entitlements.

Countries that are ranked very high on the SIGI with respect to gender discrimination are also those that WHO surveys report to have very high levels of VAWG. These countries include Afghanistan, Guinea, and Bangladesh, which all have very high levels of gender discrimination across the five indexes and a very high proportion of women subjected to physical or sexual violence by a current or former intimate partner in the previous 12 months: 46.1 percent of women for Afghanistan, 43.5 percent of women for Guinea, and 50.7 percent of women for Bangladesh.

The relationship between gender discrimination and VAWG is subject to change and should be contextualized for each society. Since national data and indicators assessing gender inequality or discrimination in a country have limited utility in revealing short- to medium-term changes because new data collection is infrequent and indicators do not reflect subnational variations, it is preferable to use international reporting mechanisms. For example, it is possible to analyze this relationship using CEDAW state party and nongovernmental country "shadow reports," as well as through UN Human Rights Council Universal Periodic Reviews. Based on such analyses, we know that sustained or sudden increases in gender discrimination and inequality over a short period of time result in increased VAWG, especially when accompanied by escalating discrimination against other groups at risk of exclusion, such as ethnic or religious minorities or indigenous people. For instance, a common factor across the varied contexts of sexual violence in conflict situations affecting women, girls, men, and boys is that they take place against a backdrop of gender-based discrimination. These dynamics affirm that efforts to foster equality and build gender-responsive and inclusive institutions are central to eliminating VAWG. Above all, very high levels of gender discrimination and VAWG reveal the causal role of gendered norms in influencing the use of violence. In this sense, gender discrimination is both an enabling condition for and an early warning sign of VAWG.

Is VAWG less likely in countries with greater gender equality between women and men?

Across the globe, there have been considerable advances in applying CEDAW in the development of pro-gender-equality laws and policies. Gender inequality is seen to be both the core of the problem and at the heart of the solution. A country free of violence against women and their children is a country where women are safe, respected, valued, and treated as equals in private and public life. There is no country in the world that has yet achieved that aspirational milestone; however, some come closer to it, such as the Scandinavian countries. While it is essential to look at reporting on VAWG to determine its prevalence, it must be understood that reports of VAWG are not the same as actual VAWG. For instance, VAWG among the groups subject to most systemic discrimination and exclusion may not be reported at all. Thus, analyzing reports may not reveal which groups and locations have the highest prevalence of violence. This gap between actual and reported VAWG can prevent us from understanding the full scope and magnitude of the problem. Moreover, countries with greater gender equality—as defined through women's economic participation and opportunity, educational attainment, health and survival, and political empowerment, among other things— may have more effective reporting institutions and often register high levels of reporting of VAWG resulting from greater societal awareness of VAWG as a social problem. For example, according to International VAW survey, in 2003 Australia registered one of the highest percentages of women subjected to sexual violence by persons other than an intimate partner since age 15 (27 percent of the population),[1] compared with just 4.4 percent of women in Bangladesh in 2004.[2] However, we know from a variety of research that gender discriminatory norms and gender inequalities are currently greater in Bangladesh than in Australia, and that they constitute significant barriers to women's awareness and capacity to report violence.

Given this, survey research examining attitudinal acceptance or justification for VAWG may serve as a better indicator of societal levels of VAWG than surveys that record actual acts of violence. This is particularly the case given the limited awareness of some forms of VAWG, such as the classification of sexual assault and harassment as violence, and the limited laws and institutions for prohibiting and reporting VAWG in some countries. A useful tool to consider in this context is the

World Values Survey, which utilizes nationally representative surveys in almost 100 countries in order to understand the attitudes, values, and motivations of different populations. A 2019 multivariate analysis of World Values Survey data found that both sexism and the acceptance of general violence in social relationships were positively related to acceptability of intimate partner violence.[3] Countries like Mali, Serbia, and India scored some of the highest ratings by men on the justifiability of a man beating his wife, compared to some of the lowest scores for this attitude in Canada, Norway, and Italy. These findings are a useful indicator of the role of patriarchal and sexist attitudes toward women in driving VAWG.

What is the role of gendered power and politics in VAWG?

Violence against women and girls is an expression of both power and powerlessness. It is used by perpetrators to assert their power—both oppressive and repressive—over women and girls. In many societies, gendered power relations make it possible to abuse women and girls without consequences, even in places where there are laws and policies intended to prohibit, prosecute, and prevent such violence. In many ways, the use of violence acts as inherent recognition of the agency and power of women and girls; when an individual or group is already oppressed and without choices, violence is not needed to keep them in their place or to express power.

Gendered power has multiple sources. While power is not zero sum, it is possible for there to be win/win outcomes; how much you have depends upon how much others have. Feminist theorist Juliet Mitchell views power as the combination of a broad array of power sources in, for instance, education, the family, religion, the economy/workplace, the political sphere, and social relations via their meaning and reinforcement.[4] Efforts to promote gender equality can redistribute women's access to the institutional sources of power without, however, removing the hierarchies of power within those institutional sites that sustain gender discrimination.

Violence against women is a major factor constraining women's participation in political life and leadership roles, thus reinforcing gendered power hierarchies. This is because violence against women does not end when women acquire formal political power. Rather, women who stand up and speak out politically, whether as candidates or just as politically active individuals, are often seen as transgressing traditional gender norms (perhaps also religious, ethnic, and caste norms), and as a result they often become targets of explicit political violence and harassment.

Acts of violence against women with public profiles have been reported in most places in the world, representing a global pattern of this form of VAWG. For example, the Afghan Human Rights Commission has monitored the murder of women politicians in Afghanistan as Taliban insurgents have increased their presence in the country. Likewise, in India, Pakistan, and Sri Lanka, there have been numerous documented cases in recent years of the harassment, beating, murder, and suicide of political women. Perhaps the most notorious instance of such violence in recent times occurred in the United Kingdom, when Labour politician Jo Cox was assassinated in 2016 as she was preparing to meet with her constituents. An incident of similar caliber occurred in Kenya, when aspiring MP Ann Kanyi was beaten, threatened, and publicly stripped in a backlash against the new constitutional gender quota that required no gender to have more than two-thirds of parliamentary seats.

Women human rights defenders (WHRDs) can also become targets of violence. They face all of the same risks as human rights defenders generally, as well as added gender-specific threats and violence. These forms of violence can have adverse social consequences, such as stigmatization and discrimination, which in turn increase the likelihood of further VAWG. Attacks against WHRDs, for instance, are often focused on their reputation and/or their sexuality as nonconforming with dominant stereotypes of appropriate female or male behavior. In 2017 Front Line Defenders recorded that 44 WHRDs were killed, which marked an increase from 40 killed in 2016 and 30 killed in 2015.[5] Likewise, following the 2016 peace agreement between the Colombian government and FARC, a nonstate insurgent group, 104 women former combatants and human rights defenders were killed as a result of the lack of security guarantees (particularly to protect women) by the state in post-conflict areas.[6]

Potential perpetrators of violence against politically active women include political opponents and criminals, community and religious leaders, state security forces and police, and media and social media commentators. Indeed, perpetrators are often party colleagues or family members of the woman, so that she confronts violence in both the public and private realms. This violence prevents women from exercising their political rights as women by sending the message that women as a group should not participate in politics.

Paradoxically, in some contexts better political representation for women can lead to new forms of abuse. As women's presence in political decision-making increases, so too does the violence against politically active women. Women's increased political voice and visibility in traditionally male-only spaces may threaten those concerned with preserving the status quo, eliciting backlash in the form of VAWG as a means to slow down societal change. This violence is much more widespread and underreported than other types: a recent International Parliamentary Union survey of 55 female politicians in 39 countries found that 82 percent had experienced psychological abuse, 44 percent had experienced death or rape threats to themselves or their children, 26 percent had experienced physical violence, and 22 percent had experienced sexual violence. These attacks can be viewed as a form of gender discrimination perpetrated against politically active women *because* they are women.

Violence against politically active women also includes sexual harassment, rape, and sexual exploitation. In early 2016 a 14-year-old girl was kidnapped from her home and raped as revenge for her mother's victory in Indian local elections. In Sudan, WHRDs are often sexually assaulted and told that they face ongoing harm if they continue their activities. In Tanzania, female judges and activists have exposed widespread practices of "sextortion," whereby women have been forced to perform sexual favors as a condition for their advancement in the public service and political party ranks.

Psychological abuse against women in public life is also rife. Death and rape threats, stalking, character assassination, and social boycotts are all popular examples; as expressed by former Australian prime minister Julia Gillard in 2016: "[T]hreats of violent abuse, of rape, are far too common. . . . A woman in public view may expect to receive them almost daily."[7] In an attempt to defame women, accusations that a woman is a bad wife, mother, or daughter—or a lesbian—may be spread through rumors or posted online, negatively affecting both her political prospects and her personal life. Where access to social media is widespread, cyber harassment involving sexual objectification and sexist insults may take a major toll on women's personal and professional lives. Gillard argues that the connection between online abuse and physical violence is real, that women feel and fear it, and that it is preventing women from standing up and serving in public life.

5

CONFLICT-RELATED VAWG

Is VAWG inevitable during war and armed conflict?

No, it is not. Yet VAWG appears to have always been a part of warfare. Historically, VAWG during war and armed conflict has been viewed as the "spoils of war," in the sense that it followed from the killing of enemy men and the looting and pillaging of enemy property. For instance, in Homer's *The Illiad*, a part-historical, part-mythical poem about the Trojan War, the abduction of Helen of Troy serves as the main storyline; however, in Pat Barker's retelling of that story, *The Silence of the Girls*, women and girls are raped and enslaved en masse by the Greeks. While fictional, these storylines show the commonplace occurrence of VAWG in the context of armed conflict, a message that is still very much applicable today.

Sexual and gender-based VAWG (as well as against men and boys) has become a characteristic of civil wars and the "new wars" that have occurred since the end of the Cold War. Most commonly, rape and sexual violence against women are associated with armed conflict, bringing to mind the Rwandan genocide and Yugoslav war in the 1990s as key examples. Arguably, however, these conflicts represented the end of a century marred by VAWG in conflict. Consider, for example, the Rape of Nanking, which involved mass rape and killings by imperial Japanese soldiers in the Second Sino-Japanese

War (1937–1945); the mass rapes by Red Army soldiers in 1945 during and after the Battle of Berlin at the end of World War II; and the My Lai massacre in March 1968 and other mass atrocities by US troops during the Vietnam War (1955–1975). Unfortunately, it appears this culture of violence has carried into the 21st century, as VAWG continues to dominate conflicts in Afghanistan, Syria, and Myanmar.

Scholars and researchers have begun to scrutinize both VAWG as well as sexual and gender-based violence perpetrated against men and boys to understand why it happens and whether it can be stopped. One approach has been to look at conflict situations in which VAWG doesn't occur at all, or at the very least does not occur in the same way or to the same extent, such as among the YPG and YPJ, the Kurdish People's Protection Units, which have ties to the Kurdistan Workers Party (PKK), or the Tamil Tigers (LTTE) insurgency in the Sri Lankan civil war (1983–2009). Investigating this phenomenon may allow researchers to extrapolate from certain conflict contexts and devise a strategy to reduce and/or prevent conflict-related VAWG. Indeed, this approach has helped to promote a global norm prohibiting sexual and gender-based violence as a weapon of war, but it is somewhat limited by the fact that VAWG has been documented in most modern conflicts and is frequently heightened and worsened in conflict situations compared to peacetime. This increase is related not only to direct warfare but also to the associated conditions of a war economy and an environment that lacks law and order. In such conflict-affected and displacement situations, women's and girls' severe lack of access to social and economic resources (which is often already poor and/or unequal prior to the outbreak of war) increases their vulnerability to violence in all its forms, be it rape, abduction, sex or labor trafficking, slavery, forced and early marriage, intimate partner violence, or sexual harassment. Likewise, it has been suggested that the presence of gender norms that prevent VAWG from being reported or recorded operates as one of the starkest indications of how widespread these types of violence are in a society. For instance, in places where homosexual sex is criminalized, men and boys may never come forward to report sexual violence for fear of persecution and legal consequences. Gender-based violence is not inevitable during war and armed conflict, but it is a pervasive pattern affecting all groups, albeit often unequally.

Is rape and other sexual violence in armed conflict an exceptional form of VAWG?

Scholars and researchers are divided on this question. Some see sexual violence perpetrated during conflict as a distinct type of violence that is qualitatively different from rape that occurs in times of peace and stability. Others see sexual violence in conflict as part of a continuum of gender-based VAWG also affecting men and boys, which is often exacerbated during conflict but must be seen in relation to VAWG in peacetime and pre- and post-conflict settings. Still others consider gender-based violence a distinct type of violence in itself and argue that it is just as deadly as war/conflict; for example, the Asia Foundation has stated that gender-based violence kills more women across the Asian region than armed conflict.[1] The difficulty of adjudicating this debate is that all three positions have some truth to them. Violence against women and girls is a part of conflict dynamics, though it may take particular forms. Unlike when considering violence in peacetime, it is important to understand the connections between gendered violence before and after armed conflict and between micro interpersonal violence and macro intergroup violence. Above all, however, as stressed by the third position, VAWG is underrecognized and underrepresented in global patterns of violence.

Over the past 20 years the study of conflict-related VAWG has generated significant new knowledge. We now know that sexual violence in conflict, particularly rape, is sometimes ordered under a clear military or armed group command directive, but at other times its occurrence appears to be random and opportunistic. We know that it affects men and boys to a greater extent than previously understood and than reported levels. What counts as a war crime, crime against humanity, or crime of genocide is still largely determined by existing gendered norms in legal precedents, social stigmas, and political contexts within individual countries. These contexts influence *who* is willing and able to report crimes and *how* they are categorized and recorded. Our awareness of which types of VAWG we see as conflict is also deeply rooted in subconscious gender bias and discrimination.

What is important to note, however, is that in a conflict situation the power of VAWG relative to other types of violence derives not from the physical violence but rather from the stigma that victims bear and that shames and oppresses whole families and communities. Physical, psychological, sexual, or economic VAWG, as discussed in chapter 1, intends to denigrate and silence victims and, by association, their wider circles. It both exploits and reinforces stereotypes and oppression based on gender, ethnicity, class, caste, sexuality, and other identities. Therefore, in an ethnic or religious conflict, VAWG may be an effective weapon or tactic in achieving the goals of the group. However, it may not be an exceptional form of violence given the entrenched patterns of VAWG before, during, and after conflict.

How and why do state and nonstate parties to a conflict perpetrate sexual violence, and does it count as VAWG?

As mentioned, sexual violence does not occur only in civil wars, nor is it only perpetrated by nonstate actors. State militaries may use sexual and gender-based VAWG as well as violence against men and boys as a strategy of political domination designed to control and repress a minority group and acquire its land and resources. In contexts where women's and girls' bodies and dress become symbolic of group identity and difference, particularly in ethnic, nationalist, and extremist groups, controlling women's mobility and public participation contributes to the dynamic of intergroup conflict. Countries with conflict-related sexual violence documented by the UN Security Council are also countries where women's political voice and access to public space are severely constrained. We can see this relationship unfold in the recent political uprising in Sudan, where women experienced systematic sexual assaults by military forces during protests. Indeed, while women were among the most visible leaders of the protest movement in Sudan in 2019, in the aftermath and transition to a new regime, their political leadership has been sidelined.

Conflict-related VAWG perpetrated by nonstate armed actors is extremely common but often goes unreported, as there are simply no available institutions to respond to the violence. Some may deduce from this that the violence doesn't happen, which can lead to the assumption that only state militaries are perpetrators of VAWG. There are strong in-group incentives to focus on the violence perpetrated by the enemy group and to ignore any violence or violations within the group. For instance, you may be considered a traitor for reporting people from your own group. Or you may consider certain types of in-group violence acceptable but secondary to major conflict, such as forced abortions in the FARC during its armed insurgency in Colombia. In some circumstances, the political fight for ethnic and religious autonomy may not permit reports of human rights violations against women within the nonstate armed group. Furthermore, reports and rumors of sexual violence perpetrated by a state military may be used to fuel recruits to nonstate armed groups and advance their insurgency in the name of "protecting our women." In Myanmar, for instance, ethnic minority groups have posted photos of victims of rape committed by the Burmese Tatmadaw state military on social media as a means to mobilize and generate support for retaliation. In this sense, both nonstate and state actors have used sexual violence and other forms of gender-based violence during conflict, sometimes as part of a war-fighting strategy and sometimes as a result of the climate of impunity that is prevalent during armed struggles.

What are current international approaches to stopping rape and other VAWG in war?

Women's rights advocates have fought for decades for the recognition of rape and other VAWG in war as crimes. Beginning at the UN Human Rights Conference in Vienna in 1993, activists facilitated witness testimony from victims of sexual and gender violence, notably from World War II Korean and Filipina comfort women. At the same conference, activists drew upon the extreme violence perpetrated against women during conflict in the former Yugoslavia to push for the recognition of gender-based violence as a human rights violation, not merely an incidental outcome of conflict.

Then, later in the decade, women's movements brought women victims and survivors to the International Criminal Tribunals on Former Yugoslavia and Rwanda. As a result of this advocacy in the Women's Caucus for Gender Justice, in 1998 sexual violence and gender-based violence were defined as international crimes in the Rome Statute, which also established the International Criminal Court.

In October 2000 the United Nations Security Council designated for the first time a special session to discuss gender issues in international peace and security. Security Council members openly debated the impact of war and armed conflict on women, VAWG, gender issues in peacekeeping missions, the role of women in rebuilding post-conflict societies, and women's participation in peace negotiations and decision-making processes. Following this, in 2008 Security Council members recognized conflict-related VAWG as a threat to international peace and security in Resolution 1820. Importantly, this provided the language for UN peacekeeping missions with specific Security Council mandates to protect civilians from situations of widespread and systematic acts of sexual violence.

In 2009 the UN established the UN Office of the Secretary-General Special Representative on Sexual Violence in Armed Conflict. Its mandate is to document and investigate conflict-related sexual violence in various countries, bringing those of concern to the UN Security Council through an annual reporting mechanism. A UN team of expert investigators is tasked with documenting crimes, while women's protection advisers with specialized training in responding to sexual violence are embedded in UN peace operations, such as active conflicts in Africa. This office operates in tandem with CEDAW General Recommendation 30 (2010), under which states have a positive duty to protect women's human rights at all times; to advance substantive gender equality before, during, and after conflict; and to ensure that women's diverse experiences are fully integrated into all peacebuilding, peacemaking, and reconstruction processes.

Primarily, these international legal and policy frameworks aim to prevent conflict-related VAWG by identifying perpetrator individuals and groups and punishing them either through criminal prosecution and/or UN sanctions (or the threat thereof). Under international law, evidence of even one incident may be sufficient proof of a systematic pattern of violence. This approach to prevention through the deterrent effect of prosecution may also deliver a form of retributive justice to survivors whose cases may reach national or international courts. However, it should be noted that to date (2020) the prosecution of conflict-related sexual violence has been limited relative to the frequency and scale of the crime.

The UN has also prioritized measures to address perpetrators. This is visible in the legal recognition of sexual violence and gender-based violence as war crimes, the development of new protocols for investigating and documenting said crimes, new programs to train and socialize national militaries, efforts to work with nonstate armed groups to promote moral codes of conduct, and drives to ensure that peace negotiations and political deals to end conflict do not contain immunity provisions for sexual and conflict-related violence. However, to date (2020) the effectiveness of this range of prevention measures is largely untested.

Measures directly addressing the suffering of victims and access to justice have until recently been less well developed. Significant programming in conflict-affected countries has focused on addressing the stigma that survivors bear in their communities, which often shun them after the violence and, in the case of women and girls, consider them unmarriageable. These programs aim to raise awareness of the plight of female and male survivors and their experiences of violence. Namely, destigmatization involves working with communities to tell survivor stories, provide ongoing trauma counseling, and establish livelihood programs to facilitate rehabilitation and reintegration.

On a global level, there is now greater attention being paid to the voices of survivors and the value of their opinions in designing strategies to prevent conflict-related VAWG. Individual survivors have briefed the UN Security Council, and notably, the 2018 Nobel Peace Prize was awarded to both Nadia Murad, a Yazidi woman survivor who escaped ISIS enslavement including gang rape, and Denis Mukwege, a doctor and refugee who established a hospital in the DRC to help repair the bodies and lives of female survivors of conflict-related rape. Both have spoken truth to power about the scourge of rape, sexual slavery, and abuse affecting women and girls during conflict, in particular in Iraq and the DRC. Particularly powerful was the fact that Nadia Murad refused to be shamed by her victimization and chose not to cover her face when giving testimony. Likewise, Denis Mukwege stated that his goal was to transform pain into power, and that it was "the strength of women" survivors that kept his work going.

In addition to these approaches and measures to stop conflict-related sexual and gender-based violence, the UN Women,

Peace and Security agenda addresses the structure of gender inequality in peace and security institutions affecting both perpetrators and victims. In particular, an international initiative to increase the number of women serving as UN peacekeeping troops is expected to improve responses to conflict-related violence. With greater gender balance in peacekeeping forces and with peacekeepers trained in gender-responsive protection, it is hoped that more victims will report crimes; peacekeepers will be more likely to identify existing crimes and stop perpetrating them themselves; and where crimes might occur in the future, peacekeepers will ensure compliance with prohibitions against this type of violence.

Efforts to promote more gender-inclusive peace processes involving women's participation are also crucial to addressing the gendered power relations conducive to conflict-related sexual and gender-based violence. Research has shown that when women participate in elite peace processes, both formally and informally, it is more likely that there will be provisions in a final peace agreement that remove impunity for conflict-related sexual violence and gender-based violence crimes, thereby ensuring transitional justice for victims/survivors and their families. However, these peace processes also need to address sexual abuse and exploitation by UN civilian and military peacekeepers, which was described by a UN review in 2013 as the most significant risk to UN peacekeeping missions and likely remains significantly underreported.[2]

Finally, improving local and national institutions and eliminating discriminatory processes for reporting violence is a crucial prevention measure that both sends a message to perpetrators and facilitates victim voice and justice. While reporting is primarily used for the purpose of data gathering, prosecution, and prevention through deterrence, it may also be used to deploy early warning prevention programs and conflict prevention initiatives, as well as to support gender parity in peace processes.

Part 2

CAUSES OF VAWG

6

MEN, MASCULINITIES, AND VAWG

How does masculinity affect VAWG?

Why is it the case that men perpetrate the vast majority of all VAWG? While not all men commit this violence, being a man is a significant risk factor for the perpetration of VAWG. Some evolutionary accounts see violence and aggression as natural behaviors for men who are otherwise constrained by modern institutions. However, a better argument is that masculinity is in fact dynamic (rather than fixed by biology or any other factor), and that it is the social constructions of masculinity within and across almost all societies that have encouraged and rewarded male aggression and violence toward themselves and others.

Adapting Simone de Beauvoir's famous expression with regard to the achievement of womanhood, one is not born, but rather becomes, a man. In most societies, the achievement of manhood is precarious; it needs to be continually performed through public demonstrations of dominant attributes of masculinity. Boys and men are often asked to "be a man" or "man up" and avoid any show of emotion except anger. Even when explicit physical violence is punished, men and boys are encouraged to be physically strong and rough and to play contact sports, in which the threat of violence is implicit. The question for any given society is: Which attributes and behaviors need to be performed to be accepted as a man?

When men are socialized to conform to traditional gender roles as breadwinners, leaders, soldiers, and so on, and to meet conventional gendered expectations that a man should be strong, dominant, and rational, they may be socialized to hold gender inequitable attitudes that either directly or indirectly support VAWG. In this way, the social constructions of aggressive masculinities and silent femininities are root causes of VAWG. Dominant forms of masculinity in particular help to maintain the privilege and power that men as a group hold over women as a group. This structure of gender inequality makes coercive control more likely, whether through physical, psychological, or economic violence over women and girls. In this sense, socialized forms of masculinity can promote the acceptance and spread of VAWG.

Why do some men and not others perpetrate VAWG?

Since masculinity intersects with identities based on age, race, ethnicity, religion, socioeconomic status, sexuality, and ability, among others, there are multiple masculinities and different experiences of being a man. Men who experience structural discrimination and disadvantage by virtue of these identities, and who are unable to attain the status and power of other men, may use violence to achieve a sense of power. Crucially, though, this assertion of power is often exercised in and through acts of VAWG.

Psychologists and public health practitioners often stress the individual risk factors that determine which men perpetrate VAWG. These factors include excessive alcohol consumption, childhood experience of witnessing or being subject to violence, and/or the presence of a mental health condition. However, these individual risks also interact with learned gender norms and behaviors. For instance, Michael Flood's research has shown that boys who have been victims of violence are more likely than girl victims to use or support violence as adults. These gender norms about violence are often learned in male-dominated settings, such as families, bars, schools, sports clubs, and certain professions, and enforced by other men, including fathers, brothers, and friends.

Research indicates that men and boys who hold and adhere to more traditional attitudes regarding masculinity are also more likely to hold attitudes that are gender inequitable and supportive of violence, which is conducive to VAWG. In social surveys, one of the best predictors of an individual's attitudes toward VAWG is his or her level of support for gender inequality. These findings suggest explicit links exist between dominant norms of masculinity and VAWG, and that a rigid attachment to these norms increases the likelihood that men will hold sexist attitudes and be prone to perpetrating or justifying VAWG. Thus, men who hold fixed ideas about gender and about what it means to be a man may find it difficult to change their violent behaviors—whether those behaviors relate to VAWG or to other forms of violence, such as gun violence and extremist or terrorist violence. The violence perpetrated by "incels" is a case in point and can be classified as both explicitly gender-based and terrorist. Incels, including the 25- and 22-year-old men behind attacks in Toronto and Santa Barbara, respectively, have randomly killed civilian women based on their grievance against a system that they perceive as having failed to enable them to have sexual access and conquest over women, mimicking other extremist political causes.

It is challenging to think that some violence that does not appear on its face to be gendered or a form of VAWG but is perpetrated mostly by men might actually be gender-based. Gender norms are inextricable from the norms that regulate violent conflict. For instance, the honor code still practiced in some societies has enabled men's violence inside and outside of traditional conceptions of war, while the gender norm of women's seclusion has limited women's direct participation in violence. In terms of the honor code, male family members are expected to protect female family members to uphold the honor of the family unit. In societies where this norm is in place, men are empowered to retaliate with violence against any person who threatens the piety of the female member, including the female member herself if she transgresses social codes of conduct, such as by leaving the home without a male guardian or interacting with a male who is not a family member (outside of marriage). In a study by Elin Bjarnegård, Elin, Karen Brounéus, and Erik Melander, men who subscribe to such an honor code and who oppose gender equality were found to be four times more likely to use violence in political uprisings than those not embracing the honor code. The upshot of this study is that gender equality has a pacifying effect on masculinity and on the use of political violence.

Is VAWG perpetrated by men and boys only?

While the patterns of VAWG are gendered, and men and boys are perpetrating most of this violence, some women are also perpetrators of violence, including against women and girls. While very uncommon, maternal filicide (mothers killing their children) is one such example. A 10-year study of maternal filicide in the Australian state of Victoria conducted by Thea Brown and colleagues found that severe depression was the most common cause, with substance abuse and domestic violence as contributing factors.[1] Compared with paternal filicide, when mothers kill their children, they typically have altruistic or neglectful motivations associated with severe depression, an existing mental illness, low income, and other poverty-related stressors but no previous history of child abuse. Women may also act violently toward female intimate partners, and though the evidence is inconclusive, same-sex couples including lesbian couples tend to have a comparable or slightly higher risk of intimate partner violence than heterosexual couples. Battered women syndrome is relatively common and a legitimate legal defense in many countries, used by women who kill their (usually male) intimate partners in response to systematic domestic violence.

We know women perpetrate violence—including against other women and girls—but overall to a far lesser extent than men. Indeed, there have been situations of conflict, genocide, and terrorism in which women have been known to commit atrocities against civilian women, girls, men, and boys. Mia Bloom cites the case of Samira Ahmed Jassim, who coordinated the rape of 80 young women so she could recruit them to serve as suicide bombers for Ansar al Sunnah in Iraq.[2] Similar evidence of women affiliated with the Islamic State who were involved in sexual violence and slavery of Yazidi women is now also emerging. Sara E. Brown shows in her study of the 1994 Rwandan genocide that women played a central role in acts of violence against Tutsi; almost 2,000 women convicted of genocide-related crimes remain in Rwandan prisons.[3] Most famously, the Rwandan minister of family affairs and women's development at the time, Pauline Nyiramasuhuko, was the first woman convicted of genocide by an international court and sentenced to life in prison for her part in the massacre. Many ordinary women were also convinced to encourage the perpetration of violence by propaganda that caused divisions among women. However, conforming to gendered expectations, women committed significantly fewer acts of overt violence and killing than men during the Rwandan genocide. Those women who do perpetrate VAWG frequently take on masculine attributes in their performance of power and are often rejected as women or seen as unfeminine or unmotherly.

Are men and boys themselves victims of sexual and gender-based violence?

Gender-based violence against men and boys is a problem. Sometimes, gender binary approaches that highlight VAWG may unintentionally render the victimization of men and boys invisible. Sexual violence perpetrated against men and boys may include a range of heinous acts, including anal and oral rape, genital torture, castration, and coercion to rape others.

Many of these acts are seen as emasculating and as a result have received little attention until recently. Furthermore, LGBTQI+ men who do not identify with binary gender constructs can be subject to abuse by other men who perceive them as less manly or effeminate. Institutional violence against men and boys is also rife, including the sexual abuse of boys in orphanages, at schools, in clubs such as the Boy Scouts, and in religious institutions such as the Catholic Church. Sadly, these types of abuse have come to public attention only over the past two decades, meaning their prevalence and impact remain underexplored.

Generally speaking, gender-based violence perpetrated against men and boys is probably even more unknown and underreported than that against women and girls. As well as enduring the shame and stigma that attach to all victims of sexual and gender-based violence (and lead them to stay silent), masculine gender norms encourage men and boys to endure the abuse. Moreover, the assumption that male victims are homosexual, when homosexuality is still criminalized in a number of states in the world today, leads many boys and men to refrain from reporting these crimes for fear of being prosecuted themselves. In conflict situations, male survivors' accounts may be reported but then recorded by investigators as acts of torture rather than incidences of sexual violence against men. Elise Feron argues that men's experiences of violence are desexualized, while women's experiences of sexual violence are depoliticized.[4] In her book, she estimates that in Syria and Eastern Congo, up to one-third of all victims of sexual violence are men and boys. Overall, underreporting of gender-based violence against men and boys makes it difficult to develop appropriate responses to these crimes.

Can men help other men to stop perpetrating VAWG and change their behavior?

Men can challenge the dominant attributes of masculinity and engage with other men and boys to challenge gender norms and promote nonviolence and positive, respectful masculinities. Most men do not perpetrate VAWG; these men as well as those who have changed their behaviors and attitudes may be influential in preventing other men from abusing women and girls. For example, VAWG bystander effect studies have found that men are more likely to intervene as bystanders to an act of VAWG or to other men displaying sexist or violent behavior when their attachment to masculine norms is weaker.

Men can also lead other men and their male relatives, especially their sons, in role modeling nonviolent, nonaggressive behavior and alternative ways to be a (good) man. White Ribbon is one of the most famous men's organizations; started in Canada as a result of an egregious act of male violence, it has subsequently diffused around the world with distinct country branches and campaigns, especially during the 16 Days of Activism against Gender-Based Violence. Similarly, Promundo and Sonke Gender Justice are two global organizations, in Brazil and South Africa respectively, founded to engage men and boys in gender equality and the prevention of violence against women. Both are connected to the MenEngage movement, and their approach is to transform gender norms by challenging dominant and rigid forms of masculinity and promoting feasible, alternative models. This is important, as some anti-VAWG programs can actually reinforce norms and gendered power that is conducive to VAWG by appealing to men to "man up" or act as real men who can protect women and girls from violence. It is only by challenging these norms that successful and lasting behavior change around VAWG can occur.

7

CULTURE AND VAWG

Is the recognition of VAWG universal or culturally relative?

Violence against women and girls presents itself in different forms across all cultures. Culture itself is a dynamic and changing concept. Within various cultures both the recognition and the prevalence of VAWG depend on who holds the power and resources to shape and define cultural ideology in educational, religious, and media institutions and/or on the core principles of the culture. Culture is not a static or unchanging entity against which violations of women's human rights or VAWG can be assessed; rather, it is a negotiated and continually contested set of social practices influenced by the power and status of key interlocutors who participate in and interpret these practices. When people question whether a cultural practice or an apparent tradition negatively affecting women and girls is a form of VAWG (such as FGM/C or honor killings) and suggest that we need to respect different cultures, we need to ask: *Whose* culture and tradition do we respect? Who speaks for practices that circumscribe women's basic freedoms and capabilities? When women's voices are at the center of the debate between the universality of human rights and the relativity of culture, the complexity of the cultural argument is revealed.

Arati Rao argues that "no social group has suffered greater violation of its human rights in the name of culture than women."[1] Culture is bound up in social relations and historical formations that often oppress women, such as men's exclusive leadership of religion and religious teachings that permit wife-beating and other practices considered to be VAWG. For example, in Pacific Island cultures, forms of VAWG are sometimes condoned under traditional forgiveness practices, as well as traditions of early, arranged, or forced marriages and informal adoptions.

No matter its form in different societies, the concept of culture circumscribes women's lives in tangible and symbolic ways. Traditionally women have been seen as the guardians of culture and, given their role as primary caregivers, the earliest inculcators of culture in children. Women's dress and appearance make them visible and vulnerable embodiments of culture. As a result, states and other collectivities have developed agendas to control women, as demonstrated by specific policies that regulate their reproductive capacities and curtail their freedom of movement, family status, and civil rights.

The conception of culture frequently referred to by international actors is falsely rigid, ahistorical, and selectively chosen. We must ask: Whose interests are being served, and who benefits from such a conception? Women and girls have become instrumentalized in political, economic, military, and discursive battles within and between societies. Indeed, the international human rights movement is itself part of the problem, with its conceptual gender biases at the policy level and its focus on the public sphere as the primary site of human rights violations, at the expense of violations in the private sphere. Cultural defenses of VAWG in the developing and developed world should be critically scrutinized. Women are neither pure victims nor beneficiaries of culture in any country or location; it is only by recognizing women's limited access and rights to determine cultural practices that we can begin to place culturally relativist arguments that justify forms of VAWG in social and political context.

How and why are some forms of VAWG justified?

The anti-VAWG movement has identified several practices embedded in systems of kinship and marriage as instances of gender-based violence. These practices are often described as cultural practices and are normatively supported as such, in the sense that they are seen as socially desirable acts that promote moral and modest behavior in women. However, most of these practices are designed to safeguard, restrict, and control women's sexuality, reproductive capacities, and autonomy. For example, FGM/C, which is practiced across Africa, Asia, and the Middle East, is legally banned in many countries. Despite this, it is estimated that more than three million girls are at risk of undergoing the practice every year. For instance, Egypt banned the practice in 2008, yet over 90 percent of Egyptian girls and women aged 15–19 have undergone it.[2] Traditionally, it is older women who perform FGM/C on young girls, and many women are strong supporters of the practice. Thus, women's agency and victimization are tied up in this act of VAWG.

This practice has been a deep-rooted norm, and a number of cultural beliefs contribute to its significance in many societies. First, FGM/C is seen as a tradition and social obligation that brings honor to the girl and her family. Cutting diminishes sexual drive and presents the girl as chaste, marriageable, and faithful. Moreover, cultural cues reinforce its social significance: uncut girls may not be allowed to serve or prepare food because they are considered unclean. Farage and coauthors (2015) discuss how friends and peers who have undergone FGM/C may make fun of uncut girls or ostracize them from social groups. Colloquial, derogatory smears reinforce the opinion that remaining uncut is shameful.

Second, while practiced by various religions and nonreligious groups alike, FGM/C is often a religious obligation in chiefly Muslim communities. That being said, governments and religious leaders have recently begun campaigning against FGM/C.

Third, external genitalia are considered unclean and unsightly in some societies; in particular, the clitoris and/or labia minora can be perceived as belonging to male bodies or as body parts to be bled to cleanse and purify.

Fourth, FGM/C is viewed as a rite of passage that reinforces cultural identity and group belonging. For instance, in countries such as Liberia, Sierra Leone, Guinea, and the Ivory Coast, it occurs as part of a group initiation into secret women's societies. In these settings, FGM/C forms part of a wider set of gendered cultural practices; the event occurs in private, often performed by a woman community leader, and girls will spend up to several weeks away from home learning about the norms and responsibilities of womanhood. The practice can also be culturally reinforced; public recognition, community celebrations, and the showering of gifts upon girls cultivate a sense of identity and pride. This affirmation even extends to wider social circles, with female relatives looked upon favorably by communities for performing their duty.

Another example of a cultural practice that is also a form of VAWG is honor killings. An honor killing is an act of vengeance, usually resulting in death, perpetrated by family members (particularly fathers or brothers) against female family members for bringing dishonor on the family (for instance, by engaging in sex outside of marriage or being suspected of doing so). It is part of a larger category of crimes justified by the need to conserve male and family honor by controlling women's sexual conduct and perceived inappropriate conduct. These "crimes of honor" regulate the expression of women's sexuality and are viewed as a culturally imbued method of maintaining a family's reputation and the boundaries of a community and its intergenerational reproduction.

In this sense, they are similar to crimes of passion: in both situations, VAWG is justified by a man's rage at finding out (or merely being suspicious of) a women's sexual engagement with another, which is seen to bring dishonor.

A cultural justification for honor killings arises where family honor is contingent on men's courage and women's sexual modesty; in this sense, failures by individual men or women result in harm to the entire family. For instance, in some societies, if a woman acts immodestly or partakes in extramarital sex, she is perceived to bring humiliation and disgrace not only upon herself but also upon her family. The killing of the woman thus serves as a means of preservation for the family's honor and ensures relief from the slurs and attacks of others. Honor killings are often perceived to be justified by Islamic religious doctrine. Importantly, however, the practice is not supported in the religion, nor is its incidence restricted to Muslim-majority countries. As the UN Special Rapporteur on Extrajudicial, Summary or Arbitrary Executions has noted, "a number of renowned Islamic leaders and scholars have publicly condemned the practice and clarified that it has no religious basis."[3]

Why is there a culture of silence and stigma around VAWG?

Some cultures promote silence around VAWG, and the silence of victims can be perpetuated due to gender norms within the dominant cultural frameworks of a society, inadequate legal protections, and a culture of impunity around VAWG. For example, there are continued high prevalence rates for both FGM/C and early marriage in Nigeria. According to the 2013 Nigeria Demographic Health Survey,[4] approximately 25 percent of women and girls have undergone FGM/C, and 43 percent of marriages are child marriages. These high figures exist in spite of the government's creation of a legal framework for protecting women and girls and reducing these practices, as well as banning their performance in some states within the country.

The culture of silence around FGM/C and early marriage is based on gender norms that are deeply embedded in Nigerian society. They are defined by the male—and sometimes female—custodians of cultures, perpetuating the idea that gender power relationships and inequalities are natural. Research conducted by Oxfam in 2018 identified a series of gender norms that acted as drivers of FGM/C and early marriage in Nigeria. These included the ideas that a respectable woman marries early, is submissive to male authority and is not promiscuous, and is worth more as a wife than as a daughter. Women and girls who transgressed these norms faced varying sanctions, ranging from family/peer pressure and condemnation of the girl and her mother (with implications for their social acceptance and family honor) to physical exclusion or banishment from their friendships and wider communities. Finally, in extreme cases, forced FGM/C and early marriage have resulted in cases of femicide and suicide.

Considering this culture of silence in another context, southeast Myanmar, a 2018 report by the Karen Human Rights Group examined the traditional gender norms, stigma, and victim blaming surrounding sexual VAWG. Gender norms in southeast Myanmar are heavily influenced by religion; for instance, in the dominant Buddhist religion, men have a superior status to women, and women are expected to dress in a conservative way. Furthermore, women's responsibility and decision-making does not usually extend beyond the family household. In this setting, gender discrimination and inequality leads to victim blaming in incidents of VAWG, and survivors face even further discrimination and social stigma if the violence is publicly known. Furthermore, police officers and judges have shown a tendency to blame the demeanor of women in cases of sexual violence due to a widely held perception that rape only happens to women who are not respectable. Finally, virginity is regarded as sacred in southeast Myanmar. Survivors of rape are considered to bring bad luck to the community, and as men will not agree to marry rape victims, survivors may feel that they have no choice but to marry the perpetrator (with added pressure from local elders to do so).

Inadequate legal protections for survivors also reinforce the silence around sexual VAWG. Myanmar still has no VAWG-specific legislation, and the general criminal code is outdated and poorly enforced. As a result, very few survivors have meaningful recourse in law. In particular, in rural areas where armed ethnic groups operate, civilians have limited knowledge of the relevant laws and mechanisms to report crimes, which is compounded by the fact that perpetrators often threaten victims and their families to deter them from reporting or speaking out in public.

A culture of impunity for sexual violence crimes exists where there is a severe lack of trust in the security sector and justice system. In Myanmar, past and current sexual violence committed by Tatmadaw (Myanmar state armed forces) soldiers has either been disregarded or dealt with via nontransparent military justice systems, which generally shield perpetrators from further prosecution and sanctions. The official justice system is expensive, corrupt, inefficient, and gender-biased, and it operates with significant language barriers for ethnic minorities who are not proficient in Burmese. The only alternative—community-based, informal, male-led justice mechanisms—undermines victims' rights and increases the likelihood that powerful perpetrators will pressure authorities to drop charges against them.

Can we criticize other cultures, religions, and nationalities for their VAWG practices?

The use of physical and psychological violence to control women's lives has a long history in all parts of the world. In all global regions, men's efforts to control women's bodies are more likely to be tolerated than punished. Traditional harmful practices, including honor killings and FGM/C, are ultimately expressions of a patriarchal kinship system in which power and resources flow through males, and women and their reproductive capacities ensure the transfer of power and resources across generations of men.

Of course, we can criticize other cultures, religion, and nationalities to the extent that they condone or fail to protect against VAWG by treating perpetrators with impunity. However, we must also critically scrutinize our own cultures and societies, including practices we may take for granted— an example is a different form of body modification, cosmetic surgery, to meet Western standards of beauty and perceived attractiveness. If we accept culture to be a dynamic and changing concept with distinct manifestations across different places and times, then it is inappropriate to hold one culture— that is, a Western liberal view of the world—as superior and require other cultures to conform to its norms.

Moreover, some traditional harmful practices are disputed within and across cultures, and it is possible to appreciate that one person's defining ritual is another person's meaningless superstition. Indeed, with respect to other cultures and societies, criticism alone is a rather unsuccessful way to effect meaningful change; rather, it is more effective to support anti-VAWG interlocutors within different cultures and societies in ways that amplify their priorities and influence. In this sense, rather than being overly critical, campaigns and measures to address VAWG generally must be adapted for specific contexts (i.e., the specific types of VAWG and their causal factors) and promoted in the local language.

We also want to appreciate that there are many different ways to respect the rights and integrity of all women and girls and to eliminate gender-based violence, and that what works in certain cultures and nationalities may seem unsuitable in others. For instance, in some societies, a campaign by young men celebrating their mothers may be more effective in challenging traditional patriarchal norms that prescribe the invisibility and subordination of women than a campaign delinking women's sexual consent from their freedom of dress. Just as all cultures and societies experience VAWG in different ways, we cannot expect all cultures and societies to adopt the same methods in confronting VAWG and gender discrimination.

8

VAWG AND THE MEDIA

How do the media represent VAWG?

Media representations of VAWG are poor. Even if they do not explicitly blame victims, the media often objectify, sensationalize, stigmatize, or cast doubt on their credibility. Women and girls are often presented in a binary fashion as either "victims" or "whores" (especially in the case of sexual violence), "ideal" or "undeserving" targets, based on whether they fit prevailing gender stereotypes of the passive, feminine subject. Moreover, the media may portray women victims as exceptional and deviant with regard to traditional sociocultural norms that define appropriate behavior for females. In the age of #MeToo, which took social media by storm in October 2017 in response to allegations of sexual harassment and assault by Hollywood magnate Harvey Weinstein, victim blaming has become increasingly sophisticated. For instance, the legal defense team for the male perpetrator in a recent murder trial in New Zealand began by stating that they were not blaming the victim; however, the lawyers then proceeded to recount the dead victim's past sexual history, as if it were relevant and as if the victim had consented to her own murder. Such activity reflects long-standing conscious and subconscious gender biases about women and violence, in which the media are directly complicit.

Media objectification of women is connected with the normalization of VAWG. Media formats can create or reinforce unfair stereotypes that are punitive to those perceived as deviating from prescribed norms of femininity and masculinity. This can in turn normalize men's aggression or violence. To investigate this, a 2008 study by Stankiewicz and Rosselli assessed 1988 advertisements listed in 58 US magazines across several categories.[1] They found that overall, 50 percent of the sampled magazines portrayed women as sexual objects, with the number reaching 75 percent for men's magazines and 67 percent for women's fashion and adolescent girls' magazines. This reflects a widespread phenomenon that many print advertisements literally morph women's bodies into objects, which has implications for how men and boys perceive women and girls.

Beyond the problem of objectification of women, media depictions of family violence, sexual assault, and sexual harassment frequently frame the violence as a product of both men's and women's behavior. Family violence, for instance, may be treated as a relationship problem rather than a criminal act. Rape and sexual harassment are more newsworthy if they are rumored to be false allegations and/or a consequence of women's behavior. These damaging narratives can even surface in anti-VAWG domains, such is their pervasiveness and potency. For example, consider the safety campaigns and messages directed at informing women about how to avoid being a victim of male violence (e.g., do not walk home alone, do not go out late at night, do not wear revealing clothing). Implicit in these campaigns is an attitude of victim blaming that suggests that VAWG is the responsibility of women rather than of male perpetrators. Further, narratives that hold women responsible for the violence they experience undermine efforts to protect women from men's violence and to improve their access to justice.

Equally as problematic as the narrative of mutual responsibility are media representations that frame incidents of VAWG as isolated, rather than indicative of a wider societal and global problem. Specifically, neutrality and balanced reporting norms may be used to disguise a more conservative reporting agenda that opposes gender equality. Such framing fails to understand the context of gendered power relations in which this violence occurs, such as men's dominance in positions of power, the institutionalization of sexism in discriminatory laws and practices, and the pervasiveness of misogynistic attitudes across societies. These reports may serve to trivialize incidents of VAWG as random events when they fail to contextualize them within a broader pattern of gendered violence and power relations, such as with reference to the number of women killed by their male partners every day or every week.

What is the role of the media in contributing to or exacerbating VAWG?

The media do not just report on social reality, that is, "the news" or "the truth"; rather, they construct it by choosing which stories to run and whose voices to amplify. The reach of the media off- and online means that they hold genuine power to influence how people view and act upon social and political issues, including VAWG. The power of the online movements #MeToo, #BalanceTonPorc, and #NiUnaMenos is a primary example; they aggregated thousands of women's stories of physical and sexual violence and harassment, ensuring that they could not be ignored any longer.

Producers, editors, writers, commentators, sponsors, and owners involved in the production of media have great power to determine how local and global publics understand VAWG: in ways that either promote women's rights or silence women's and girls' experiences as victims and survivors. Media can either amplify a story of women's equality and human rights or diminish the role of women in society by adopting racial or gender-based stereotypes about the way women should act or react. Western media often portray women through the lens of their sex and gender roles and the stereotypes that surround these. For instance, reports on an incident of VAWG often immediately mention a woman's family role or profession as a sex worker. Media can increase the harms that women experience and blur the victim/perpetrator dichotomy by implying that the victim may be in part or wholly to blame for what has occurred to her. These problematic representations affect how perpetrators and the wider community perceive VAWG. More broadly, they compound the challenges that women victims face in reporting sexual and gender-based violence crimes, exacerbate social stigma surrounding VAWG, and increase the potential for retraumatization by police and the justice system.

For example, research conducted by Women's Media Center US in 2015 found that the reporting style of rapes on US college campuses largely disregarded the lens and experience of female survivors. Few news stories discussed the impact of the alleged crimes on the victims; rather, the coverage of US college rapes was significantly skewed toward the bylines and voices of men, with women writing less than one-third of all stories. In the Associated Press coverage of sexual assault on campuses appearing in sports sections or by sports reporters, only 1 percent of stories were bylined by women. That is not to say that male journalists cannot break stories on VAWG that are attentive to women's and girl's experiences; they can and do, as Ronan Farrow showed in his Pulitzer Prize–winning exposure of Harvey Weinstein's serial criminal sexual harassment and assault of women and girls for the *New Yorker*.[2] However, often the reporting styles of male journalists and the sheer lack of female journalists covering VAWG and gender issues exacerbate the problem through an uninformed or underinformed response to VAWG.

More ethical media reporting is needed to promote societal change toward a culture of nonviolence and gender equality. Public policy and law reform should be supported by wider public messages about the reality of VAWG, with the aim of empowering survivors. In particular, more media content that challenges gender stereotypes can provide the repeated counterstereotypic exposure that is needed to eliminate gender-based discrimination and violence. There are many positive examples of such media; for example, the campaign associated with the 16 Days of Activism against Gender-based Violence intended to challenge VAWG is one such media-driven movement that has the power to create change. Likewise, *Time* magazine's naming of the #MeToo movement silence breakers as the 2017 Person of the Year was a singular and powerful statement by a media organization in the face of other media producers who we now know attempted to suppress the Weinstein and other #MeToo stories. By encouraging more media outlets to represent VAWG news and stories in an ethical, gender-sensitive way, we can harness these events as a tool to better educate and embolden the public to oppose VAWG.

How is the proliferation of media associated with technology-based VAWG?

The proliferation of new formats of media, particularly those disseminated through social media websites and applications, has created a new wave of technology-based VAWG. This includes but is not limited to child pornography, sexting, revenge porn, and other breaches of digital trust that result in harm to women and girls. One example in particular is the rise of technology-enabled image-based sexual abuse. Image-based sexual abuse is defined as the non-consensual creation, distribution, or threat to distribute nude or sexual images (photos or videos) of a person. It also includes altered imagery or "deep fakes," in which a person's face or identifying marks appear in a pornographic photo or video, creating false images. Also referred to as revenge porn or non-consensual pornography, image-based sexual abuse is marked by the invasion of a person's privacy and violation of her or his human rights of dignity, sexual autonomy, and freedom of expression.

The phenomenon of image-based abuse is increasingly common. In 2017 the Office of the eSafety Commissioner in Australia conducted a survey of 4,122 Australians and found that 1 in 10 had experienced a nude or sexual image of themselves being distributed to others or posted online without their consent.[3] Young women aged 18–24 were among the most commonly victimized, as were indigenous Australians and those with a mobility or communicative disability. Similar results were found in an RMIT University survey in March 2019, in which of the 4,274 Australians (aged 16–49) surveyed, 20 percent reported that someone had taken or created a nude or sexual image of them without their consent, and 9 percent had experienced threats that a nude or sexual image of them would be shared.[4] When the creation, distribution, and threats to distribute a nude or sexual image were combined, it was found that more than one in five Australians had experienced at least one of these behaviors.

The motivations for this type of VAWG are complex. Nicola Henry and Asher Flynn (2019) investigated non-consensual material on 77 high-volume online websites. They found that rather than seeking revenge against the person depicted (often a woman or girl), the majority of users were motivated by sexual gratification and proving their masculinity to a sexually deviant peer network. Nonconsensual image exchanges are a medium for the construction of hypermasculinity and heteronormativity, reinforcing existing gendered power relations that normalize VAWG.

Just as with offline forms of violence, the impact of image-based sexual abuse on victims—both women and girls and men and boys—is significant. It is often used to coercively control partners, threatening victims of sexual and domestic violence to prevent them from reporting or seeking access to justice. Furthermore, its adoption as a form of bullying/harassment causes a high level of psychological and emotional distress to victims, who may fear repercussions in their employment or relationships if they speak out.

What is the role of the media in preventing and reducing VAWG?

Given the rise in online social marketing campaigns and primary health prevention information, research has begun to explore how social media and other online platforms offer survivors of VAWG venues for sharing their stories and garnering support. In particular, "hashtag activism" has allowed the global anti-VAWG community to prosper. This form of activism is forged when those who follow the same hashtag connect with others sharing a similar experience, linking relevant news sources; magnifying important stories; and exchanging knowledge, resources, and strategies with others.

Katherine Bogen and her coauthors (2019) have analyzed hashtag activism in the context of the #MeToo movement. Importantly, their research found that the #MeToo movement created an online space for community formation. The movement's discussion of personal experiences meant that individuals were able to communicate the personal nature as well as wide scope of sexual violence as a social problem, making the prevalence of violence more real for their communities and networks. More broadly, Twitter has facilitated support to survivors of trauma by raising awareness of their experiences, enabling advocacy and discussion of the global problem of VAWG in an accessible and easily navigable format.

In addition to social media, which frequently fall beyond the boundaries of state regulation, mainstream media and entertainment have been used in some cases as a means for education and social change in places where traditional VAWG activism is less tolerated. For example, television and radio dramas, animated cartoons, and popular songs can be harnessed to express and disseminate anti-VAWG messages in an entertaining and engaging way, targeting broad cross-sections of the community. In post–Cold War Romania, Oana Baluta conducted research into how one pioneering TV station, Acasă, promoted a feminist antiviolence campaign in its programming. Similar to Latin American TV stations, Acasă achieved

this by embedding soap operas watched by a primarily female audience with messages of empowerment, encouraging
reporting and action on VAWG. These soap operas promoted
both an emotional and a rational response to VAWG; they
stressed that VAWG has nothing to do with love and that it
is not just the experience of a few women. Finally, they provided information on procedures to follow in case of abuse,
including how to interact with police, and reflected on the lack
of support for victims from their families and society. In South
Africa, another exemplary entertainment-education (E-E) program against domestic violence has become a trusted and fa-
vorite TV show. First broadcast in 1999, *Soul City IV* increased
public knowledge, positive attitudes, shifts in social norms,
and a sense of self-efficacy with regard to reporting VAWG
among its audience, which numbered in the millions.[5]

However, the ability to embed anti-VAWG messages into
popular media depends upon the audience take-up of these
messages. In countries and contexts where people are unable
to access broadcast or online media, anti-VAWG messages may
go unheard. For example, significant gender gaps between
men and women in access to media and the internet exist in
Bangladesh, which may explain why a national study found
that anti-VAWG campaigns broadcast on television had little
effect on women's attitudes toward VAWG. This demonstrates
that in certain contexts, such as poor, rural, fragile, and developing countries, women's limited access to media in the first
place may impinge upon the effectiveness of such campaigns.

9

DEVELOPMENT, POVERTY, AND VAWG

Is VAWG a "developing country" problem?

Violence against women and girls is a problem everywhere, affecting women and girls of all ages, in all locations, and regardless of income level and social status. A 2013 WHO global study revealed that over 35 percent of women worldwide have experienced physical or sexual partner violence or nonpartner sexual violence.[1] However, developing countries have typically presented lower awareness of the problem, fewer institutions to report the violence to, and weaker services to respond to it, often resulting in more systemic VAWG.

In these countries, barriers to reporting VAWG and poor service provision related to VAWG reflect social norms and systems that are not responsive to women's needs. For instance, demographic and health surveys in Bolivia, Dominican Republic, Peru, Burkina Faso, Côte d'Ivoire, and Mali found that a substantial number of women did not know how or where to report violence perpetrated against them. According to the World Bank's 2014 report *Voice and Agency*, the predominant reason for not reporting was the belief that there was no use in doing so; many women also cited embarrassment about sharing their experiences with another. In Mexico, the most common reasons women gave for not reporting included a perception that the violence was insignificant (29 percent);

only 8 percent of women cited "not knowing they could press charges." Among a sample of Bangladeshi women, the most common reasons given were high acceptance of violence, fear of stigma, and fear of greater harm.

Moreover, accessing treatment and support services can be expensive relative to income in developing countries. In Uganda, for example, the average direct out-of-pocket expenditure related to an incident of intimate partner violence was estimated to be the equivalent of US$5, about one-twelfth of the average monthly income in rural areas. Likewise, a 2011 household survey in Vietnam estimated that out-of-pocket expenditures for accessing services and replacing damaged property as a result of intimate partner violence averaged 21 percent of women's monthly income.[2]

Development and VAWG are fundamentally linked. This is because women's experiences of physical violence and abuse are inextricable from their experiences of poverty, labor exploitation, limitations on their sexual and reproductive rights, and the ongoing control of their mobility by ideological actors in the family and the polity. If we want to eliminate VAWG, we must address the structural gender inequalities that are the root causes of this problem, particularly those operative in a development context.

Does VAWG increase as countries grow and with rising female formal employment?

We can examine this question in the context of an economic graphing model known as a Kuznets curve, which hypothesizes that as economies develop, market forces increase and then reduce economic inequality. The "Gender Kuznets curve" shows that middle-and high-income societies can regress on gender equality achievements, including the proportion of women in the formal labor force. In contexts of rising growth, this is possible in situations where gross domestic product (GDP) stagnates and government investment in human development is set back. A common argument in these contexts, for instance, is that labor participation supports (e.g., social protection, parental leave, state-subsidized child care, and other services) are a luxury that cannot be afforded. However, an environment that perpetuates gender inequality in access to employment and resources is an environment in which VAWG thrives.

Furthermore, women's opportunities for and participation in higher education, employment, and politics have expanded in most developing countries in recent years. While such opportunities appear to open doors to greater gender equality and women's empowerment, women and girls may also face a backlash, including an increased risk of violence, as they leave home to work or study. As women's greater participation in public life—including higher education and employment—eventually becomes the norm, violence may decrease.

Likewise, women's increasing economic independence may heighten their risk of violence. Specifically, there is a stream of literature that shows how the income generation activities of women may hurt some men's sense of entitlement and dominance as breadwinners or privileged workers. As a result, these men may become more violent in order to restore their bargaining power in the home and at work. For example, the Mahatma Gandhi National Rural Employment Guarantee Scheme (NREGS) is an Indian antipoverty program that aims to increase employment opportunities for the poor and improve women's access to the labor market. A 2015 study analyzing the relationship between female labor participation and VAWG following the implementation of NREGS revealed that increased female labor participation resulted in an increase in total gender-based violence.[3] The study also found overall increases in kidnapping, sexual harassment, and domestic violence, while dowry deaths decreased. Also in India, a 2016 study of the relationship between women's employment and domestic violence among 69,704 married women aged 15–49 found that employed women had greater levels of exposure to intimate partner violence.[4] It was suggested that when household decision-making power diverges from the traditional gender norm, the emotional costs may become high for some men, and they may turn to violence to restore their domestic dominance.

While the cited studies are indicative of the problem, this trend is not specific to India; in fact, we can see its occurrence in other developing economies throughout the world. In Nigeria, a 2017 study of 20,635 currently married women aged 15–49 found that women's engagement in income-generating activities in the previous year had increased their risk of sexual intimate partner violence.[5] Furthermore, it found a positive association between cash work and physical IPV victimization that was significantly larger for women who resided in localities with greater male approval of wife-beating. In Egypt, another middle-income developing economy, mass sexual harassment and assault of women has been rigorously documented for over a decade. A 2013 UN Women study reported that 96.5 percent of women surveyed had been physically molested—that is, touched, grabbed, or groped—by a man in a public place. The main areas in which the sexual harassment took place was on the street (89 percent) and on public transport (82 percent). The study found that perpetrators of this sexual harassment were motivated by a diverse range of factors, including their desire to enforce their dominion over women in the street and a perceived sense of sexual deprivation as a consequence of economic factors making marriage expensive and prohibitive.

How does VAWG constrain economic development?

Violence against women and girls does affect economic development, and there is evidence for this relationship. The World Economic Forum's (WEF) Global Gender Gap Index (GGGI), introduced in 2006, ranks nation-states annually on their relative gender gaps for a comprehensive set of indicators relating

to economic participation and opportunity, political leadership and representation, educational attainment, health, and
survival-based criteria. The focus is on state-level growth and
productivity, and the WEF expects states to play a central
role in removing barriers to the achievement of these goals.
Reducing VAWG is an important part of this, a view shared
by the World Bank's 2016–2023 Gender Strategy, because it can
lower costs, increase mobility, open access to certain jobs, decrease absenteeism, and improve workforce productivity by
alleviating long-term trauma and mental health issues.

The development costs of VAWG are also substantial.
Estimated costs of intimate partner violence alone are close to
the average that developing country governments spend on
primary education (from 1.2 percent to 3.7 percent of GDP).
For example, according to a 2012 UN Women study, women
exposed to partner violence in Vietnam have higher work
absenteeism, lower productivity, and lower earnings than
working women who are not beaten.[6] Likewise, a 2008–2009
National Panel Survey in Tanzania showed that women experiencing current intimate partner violence earned 29 percent
less (and those currently experiencing severe intimate partner
violence earned 43 percent less) than women who had never
been abused by a partner.[7] In Chile and Nicaragua, it has been
reported that severely abused women earned 61 percent and
43 percent less, respectively, than women who had never been
abused by a partner.[8]

The World Bank's Women, Business and the Law Group's
2019 report highlights the empirical connections that have
been made over the last decade between economic rights and
participation, prosperity, and VAWG. Women's political and
economic participation cannot be further increased without
addressing the pervasive VAWG in the home, in the public
sphere, and at work. As well as pointing to the significant economic impacts of VAW such as decreased productivity, work
hours, and increasing public services costs, the WLD report

argues that women can function more freely in society and the business world when not faced by the threat of violence.

States have also begun to assess the financial costs of VAWG to government, business, and society. To date there have been more costing studies done in developed countries than developing countries because better quality data is available. In many developing countries, social and cultural norms of acceptability of the family create a culture of silence, resulting in low disclosure, lack of services, minimal utilization of available services, and inadequate information systems. For example, a 2017 KPMG report examined the costs of gender-based violence in South Africa and its impact on economic development.[9] These costs included direct or tangible costs such as health, justice, government, household and personal business, employment, and second-generation costs, as well as indirect and intangible costs, such as pain, fear, and suffering, and social and psychological impacts of violence. The conservative estimate of the costs of gender-based violence in South Africa amounted to between 28.4 billion and 42.4 billion ZAR per year, or between 0.9 and 1.3 percent of GDP annually. In Australia, KPMG estimated the cost of VAWG in 2015–2016 at $22 billion AUD, with the cost of physical and sexual violence at an estimated $12 billion AUD and the cost of stalking and emotional abuse an estimated $10 billion AUD.[10]

If we eradicate poverty, will we also eliminate VAWG?

It is true that women of all income groups experience violence perpetrated by men. However, when women have access to productive resources and enjoy equal social and economic rights with men, they are less vulnerable to violence across all societies. Not surprisingly, countries that value women's equal participation and representation and where there are fewer economic, social, or political power differences between men and women have lower levels of VAWG. Gender-based structural inequalities affecting VAWG, such as inequalities

in inheritance and land rights and discrimination in employment and business, may differ across countries according to
their type of political economy and degree of integration with
global markets. However, generally women are more able to
protect themselves from violence and to leave violent homes
and workplaces when they have good socioeconomic and
political status. Conversely, poverty puts women and girls
in situations of powerlessness, increasing their likelihood of
being abused.

Strategies for empowering women economically, including
through self-employment, collective income-generating arrangements, formal employment, and entrepreneurial market
activity, have shown some of the best-evaluated outcomes in
terms of reducing women's future experience of violence. By
giving women greater autonomy in securing livelihoods, it is
hoped that their safety and security from violent situations can
improve. In two provinces of India, researchers Bina Agarwal
and Pradeep Panda found that ownership of land or income-
earning property by women reduced their likelihood of experiencing domestic violence by 50 percent.[11] The obverse is
also true: in Kenya, where women own less than 1 percent of
the land while performing 70 percent of agricultural labor, the
denial of equal property rights places women at greater risk of
poverty, disease, violence, and homelessness.[12] Chapter 12 discusses further the particular impact of women's access to land
and property rights on VAWG.

Bargaining theory models suggest that women's access to
economic resources increases their bargaining power, thereby
reducing violence against them. Women's bargaining power
within intimate partner relationships has been extensively
studied. For instance, Oduro, Deere, and Catanzarite compared the value of a woman's total assets with those of her
partner as a proxy for her bargaining power in Ecuador and
Ghana.[13] Their results revealed that higher women's bargaining power (a proxy for their greater share of partner
wealth) was significantly associated with lower odds of

physical violence in Ecuador, and lower odds of emotional violence in Ghana. However, consistent with the argument that women's increased employment or economic opportunity may conflict with some men's sense of entitlement as breadwinners, other research in Moldova, Ukraine, and Kyrgyzstan has found that women's higher financial power compared to male spouses was associated with greater violence against the women.[14]

The epidemiological study of poverty and VAWG in households offers mixed results. In one study in Ethiopia, for instance, emotional and sexual violence was more probable in poorer households than in the richest households.[15] However, in another study in Pakistan, poverty was not a significant predictor of VAWG, but higher levels of education reduced the risk of violence.[16] Furthermore, mixed findings emerged in a sub-Saharan African study on whether women from poor households were more likely to experience intimate partner violence than women from middle-income or rich households.[17] In Zambia and Mozambique, violence was significantly higher among women from rich households than among those from poor and middle-class households. Yet in Zimbabwe and Kenya, women from poor households were the most likely to have ever experienced spousal violence, and in Nigeria and Cameroon, women from the middle class were the most likely to have ever suffered abuse from a partner.

These results suggest that VAWG cuts across all households irrespective of poverty level or wealth status. While poverty is undoubtedly a factor in men's perpetration of VAWG, so too are changing gender norms and expectations. Thus, addressing household poverty alone will not necessarily eliminate VAWG; ending such violence requires a comprehensive approach that addresses both the gender norms and inequalities in contexts of poverty as well as those operative in contexts of relative affluence.

Can women's economic empowerment in developing countries reduce VAWG?

Increasing women's economic opportunities can be an important entry point for expanding their ability to prevent and leave violent relationships. Emerging evidence suggests that economic empowerment and social protection interventions can have significant effects on domestic or intimate partner violence. For example, in Côte d'Ivoire, a group savings intervention combined with gender dialogue group counseling led to significant reductions in women's reports of economic abuse and acceptance of wife-beating, compared with women who participated only in group savings meetings.[18] Women who attended more than 75 percent of sessions with their male partner were also less likely to report physical violence.

However, mixed results arose from analysis of data from interviews with 415 married women involved in the Intervention with Microfinance and Gender Equity (IMAGE), which offers a microfinance program with a gender-training curriculum in South Africa.[19] Although improved economic conditions for women appear to be protective against intimate partner violence, the connections with indicators for women's economic situation and empowerment were inconsistent. Yet other research is supportive of the connection between women's economic empowerment and reduced VAWG. For instance, in Uganda, a vocational training program was paired with safe spaces for young women's interactions and information on health and risky behaviors.[20] Upon evaluation, it was found to have reduced the share of young women reporting forced sex from 21 percent to nearly zero, while also increasing engagement in income-generating activities by 35 percent. Likewise, a study of young married women in rural India concluded that women's joint control over their husband's income and their financial inclusion (as indicated by bank ownership) reduced intimate partner violence, whereas women's income generation or control over their own income did not.[21]

10

EMPLOYMENT, PRECARITY, AND VAWG

What type of VAWG occurs at work?

There are several types of VAWG that can occur in the context of employment and "precarious work," which refers to work that is typically low paid, insecure (in the sense that ongoing employment is uncertain or the risk of job loss is high); lacking legal protections; and with minimal employee representation about conditions, wages, or pace of work. The International Labour Organization (ILO) recognizes that women and girls can be exposed to physical assault and violence at work, as well as a range of psychosocial risks such as verbal or non-verbal threats and abusive behaviors. These behaviors are often sexualized and rooted in unequal power relations and can include unwelcome psychological harassment, bullying, or mobbing with the aim of demeaning, embarrassing, humiliating, or abusing a person.

Sexual violence and harassment at work can combine elements of physical and psychological violence. Such violence can include unwanted comments, advances, or inferences related to sexual or romantic relations; verbal abuse; deliberate physical contact; sexual assault; and rape. For example, according to a 2016 report by the NGO Sisters for Change on women garment workers in Karnataka, India, 1 in 14 women workers had experienced physical violence, while 1 in 7 women had been raped or forced to commit a sexual act while at work.[1] Where violence was reported, action taken by the factory or police occurred in just 3.6 percent of cases, and no criminal charges were brought against perpetrators.

Sexual harassment can also take the form of a hostile working environment, an assertion attributed to US lawyer Catharine MacKinnon in her pioneering book *Sexual Harassment of Working Women: A Case of Sex Discrimination* (1979). Harassment includes conduct in the workplace that creates an intimidating, hostile, or humiliating work environment. Alternatively, quid pro quo sexual harassment refers to situations in which an employee is asked for a sexual favor and consent or refusal holds consequences for her or his employment. Violence against women and girls in the workplace can be exacerbated when women are afraid to speak out against abusers for fear of loss of employment, stigmatization, or ostracization from social groups both at work and at home. When an employer is complicit in this stigmatization, survivors are often ignored or blamed, and perpetrators are able to act with impunity.

Maternal harassment or "mobbing" is a specific form of harassment that uniquely affects women employees. It refers to situations in which a woman is harassed due to her pregnancy, childbirth, medical condition related to pregnancy or childbirth, or to family responsibilities. This type of harassment can occur as a result of requests for breastfeeding breaks or other family-friendly work arrangements and involves humiliating treatment, emotional abuse, demotion or pay cuts, relocation of place of employment, and other pressures aimed at isolating or forcing female employees to resign. According to a study conducted in 2015 in the United Kingdom by the Equality and Human Rights Commission, one in five mothers experienced harassment as a result of her pregnancy or of flexible working requests being approved.[2]

While economic violence is often considered to be a form of domestic violence rather than workplace violence, it is fundamentally interconnected with workplace VAWG. For example, economic violence has a direct impact on women's ability to work, such as preventing them from having sufficient money for bus fares to get to work or for purchasing clothing suitable for work. Moreover, sometimes violent partners break women's work tools or physically remove women from their workplaces. UN Women research indicates that women who experience domestic violence are employed in higher numbers in casual and part-time work, and their earnings are up to 60 percent lower than those of women who do not experience such violence.

Is sexual harassment a form of VAWG?

Sexual harassment is absolutely a form of VAWG, one that frequently arises in the employment context. In her book, Catharine MacKinnon argues that sexual harassment is a form of sex discrimination because the act is a product of, and produces, social inequality between women and men. It refers to the unwanted imposition of sexual requirements in the context of a relationship of unequal power. Sexual harassment of women in employment is particularly clear when male superiors on the job initiate unwanted sexual advances toward female employees in a coercive manner. It might also include sexual pressures by male co-workers and customers, especially when condoned or encouraged by employers. The material coercion behind the advances may remain implicit, or it may be explicitly communicated through, for example, firing a woman worker for sexual noncompliance or making her retention conditioned upon continued sexual compliance. Sexual harassment threatens women in their jobs; indeed, when sexual harassment has an impact on employment decisions and on the workplace environment, it is a form of employment discrimination as well as VAWG.

Sexual harassment was first successfully argued and prosecuted as a form of sex discrimination by MacKinnon in the

1986 case *Meritor Savings Bank v. Vinson*. Specifically, sexual harassment was deemed to interact with the "terms, conditions and privileges of employment" under Title VII of the Civil Rights Act of 1964, which prohibits sex discrimination. Following this successful case, sexual harassment as a form of workplace VAWG was recognized in several countries. In 1986 the United Kingdom's Sex Discrimination Act was expanded under pressure from the European Court of Justice to include sexual harassment. Similarly, in 1991 the European Commission of the EU convened a committee on the protection of the dignity of women and men at work and established a definition of sexual harassment meaning "unwanted conduct of a sexual nature, or other conduct based on sex affecting the dignity of women and men at work."[3]

Non-Western countries have also adopted definitions and legislation to prohibit sexual harassment. In 1995 the Philippines enacted the Anti-Sexual Harassment Act, which provides for a clear definition of work, education, or training-related sexual harassment and specifies the acts constituting sexual harassment. It also provides for the duties and liabilities of the employer in cases of sexual harassment and sets penalties for violations of its provisions. Similarly, in 1997 the Supreme Court of India defined sexual harassment at the workplace, as well as preventive measures and redress mechanisms, in a case popularly referred to as the *Vishaka* judgment. Specifically, the set of guidelines used by the court led to the enactment of the Sexual Harassment of Women at Workplace (Prevention, Prohibition and Redressal) Act (2013), covering all women employees, including those employed in the unorganized sector as well as domestic workers.

Nowadays sexual harassment is widely recognized across international forums as a form of workplace VAWG. In 2018 the ILO found that 65 of 80 countries had specific regulations on sexual violence and harassment in the world of work, which were most commonly defined to include either quid pro quo sexual harassment or hostile working environment.

However, just 31 of those 80 countries defined sexual harassment to include both hostile working environment and quid pro quo sexual harassment.

How does precarious employment exacerbate VAWG?

Precarious employment has a significant effect on VAWG. A defining characteristic of precariousness is that the employee, rather than the employer, bears the risks associated with the job. Certain characteristics or attributes of employees, including sex, ethnicity, age, place of origin, residency status, and language abilities can predispose them toward precarious employment. Likewise, certain industry sectors are also more commonly associated with precarious employment, especially those without union representation and those with a greater share of nonstandard work arrangements.

Precarious employment makes women more dependent and therefore less able to escape violence at work or at home. Without economic independence, it is very difficult for women to leave violent partners or to find alternatives to exploitative employers, unethical recruitment agents, and traffickers. This can result in the cycle of violence persisting.

An example of a precarious site of employment is tea plantations in West Bengal, India, as reported by the ILO in 2009–2011.[4] In one case, a woman worker who was eight months pregnant collapsed on a tea estate plantation after she was denied maternity leave; she was forced back to work by the plantation doctor and management. Denying women workers—who comprise 80 percent of workers in this sector—access to maternity rights and health rights on the plantation is a form of VAWG. More broadly, the lack of separate sanitation facilities on tea plantations makes women workers vulnerable to sexual violence, and the absence of female doctors in plantation hospitals subjects them to potential mistreatment by male doctors.

Precarious employment is often undertaken by immigrant workers, who may adopt certain cultural beliefs or gender norms that perpetuate VAWG. For example, an Oxfam inquiry into sexual violence against women farmworkers in the United States found that Latino cultural beliefs played a significant role in the prevalence of workplace sexual violence in the agriculture industry.[5] Immigrant women socialized in their home countries to be subservient to men were often reluctant or afraid to speak up against their male harassers and stayed silent about the injustices committed against them. Poverty exacerbated by gender segregation and wage gaps in the agricultural sector, as well as women farmworkers' fear of job loss, were identified as reasons for not reporting sexual violence at work.

Because precarious work makes women more vulnerable to gender-based violence, in 2019 the ILO adopted Convention 190 and Recommendation 206 on the elimination of violence and harassment in the world of work. These instruments establish a global legal framework to prevent, identify, and provide redress in cases of gender-based violence and harassment at work. All countries that are members of the ILO are expected to align their national laws and policies with Convention 190, which protects employees and all persons working irrespective of their contractual status, including volunteers, job seekers, and job applicants, whether they are in training or work and if employment is ongoing or has been terminated. It also covers individuals exercising the authority, duties, or responsibilities of an employer. Critically, the Convention includes violence and harassment occurring beyond the physical limits of the traditional workplace, such as places where workers are paid, take breaks, or use facilities; work-related trips and travel; work-related communications; employer-provided accommodation; and the commute to and from work.

How can gender equality and decent work alleviate VAWG?

Gender equality and decent work opportunities can help to alleviate VAWG in the workplace, particularly the violence and harassment associated with women's employment in precarious work situations. The possibility of workplace gender equality and decent work opportunities can help to increase earnings, improve employment prospects, and widen opportunities for advancement and skill development, providing women with greater economic independence and resources to leave situations of violence. Secure employment and benefit schemes can also help women maintain safe housing and avoid homelessness or precarious living situations in which they are more vulnerable to violence. In this sense, workplaces that champion female workers and uphold gender equality policies can effectively challenge the social narrative of the male breadwinner and male dominance. By presenting women with the opportunity to continue as income earners and as equal (and not necessarily primary) caregivers in the home, working women emerge as independent economic actors who have agency and deserve respectful relationships.

Furthermore, gender equality policies in the workplace can stop discrimination against women on the basis of pregnancy and/or other maternal leave by encouraging security of contract and equal entitlements for male and female workers. Rewarding paid care work with adequate remuneration is also an important step, as it widens the opportunities for women to participate across the workforce. Supporting women's representation, participation, and leadership in decision-making will also help to challenge occupational and sectoral segregation, which often places women in disadvantageous and disempowering positions. Notably, this is not just applicable to the corporate sector; it also applies to all areas of government and within employer and employee groups and unions. All of these things—gender equal employment policies, adequate remuneration, and supporting women's participation across economic sectors and occupations—will contribute to challenging the subordination and marginalization of women in the workplace and relatedly, the normalization of workplace VAWG by employers, business, and governments.

What is the responsibility of employers and businesses in addressing VAWG?

Workplaces are crucial environments in which to engage in actions to prevent violence against women and to support women who are experiencing or seeking to leave situations of violence. Workplaces can play an important role in helping women to remain safe, stay in work, and access specialist services. To effectively prevent VAWG, workplaces should provide legal protections that prohibit discrimination and gender-based violence in general, thereby placing the burden of proof on employers regarding VAWG. In relation to maternity and family responsibilities specifically, these protections should provide a right to return to work after leave of absence to the same or equivalent position and pay and ensure gender-specific health protection in the workplace. Equal remuneration for work of equal value is also integral to gender equality and decent work environments and should be legally embedded in all workplaces.

Actions to promote gender equality and prevent VAWG involving workplaces might include strategies such as direct participation programs for employees, in which they can act as a violence or harassment support person or adviser, or opportunities to engage in organizational and workforce development that includes awareness training on VAWG. On a smaller scale, employer communications, social marketing, and advocacy that promotes positive nonviolent relationships are important, as are employer contributions to anti-VAWG campaigns. Finally, legislative and workplace policy reform (e.g., including paid or unpaid leave for domestic violence victims) is essential to ensure that victims have strong protections and employment guarantees when dealing with violence.

Violence against women and girls at work and in the home, for instance sexual harassment and assault in the workplace and intimate partner violence, impacts both employees and the workplace, and therefore employers and businesses have a responsibility to address both forms of VAWG. According to a 2012 survey conducted by the US Society for Human Resource Management, almost 20 percent of 691 organizations surveyed reported experiencing a domestic violence incident in the previous year.[6] Anti-VAWG advocate Holly Rider-Milkovich and employment law attorney Elizabeth Bille (2019) identify three critical questions that companies need to ask themselves regarding their support of employees who may be experiencing domestic violence: What are the policies related to domestic violence in the workplace? Whose responsibility is it to address this violence? And how have they as employers made employees aware of these policies?

To exemplify best practices, employers should create and maintain a domestic violence policy that affirms their commitment to supporting vulnerable employees and addressing the safety concerns of the impacted employee and others. Indicative policies should provide information about antiviolence resources to all employees and the process the employer will follow in a domestic violence situation. They should also prohibit discrimination or retaliation against impacted employees and outline the assistance available to them. Furthermore, Milkovich and Bille recommend universal mandatory training for all employees. This shows employees that their employer cares about domestic violence and is invested in their safety and well-being, while also removing the shame and stigma attached to the situation. It is also critical for employees to know the warning signs of potential violence and how to respond to or seek assistance for harassment, given the possibility that an abuser may enter the workplace.

11

MIGRATION, HUMAN TRAFFICKING, AND VAWG

What forms of VAWG do migrant women workers most frequently experience at work?

Women and girls are increasingly on the move. In some cases, gender-based violence is pushing them to move; in other cases, they experience gender-based violence on their journey or at their destination. Regardless of where migration sits on the forced to voluntary continuum—from seeking economic livelihood and better opportunities to being trafficked, kidnapped, coerced into marriage, or displaced by family members and/or conflict—women and girls are encountering violence.

Migrant women and girls are about half of the estimated 258 million international migrants, and there are approximately 66.6 million women migrant workers worldwide. An estimated 100 million women migrant workers send remittances (money transfers) back home annually, representing half of all remittance senders globally. This is despite the facts that the wages of women migrant workers are commonly lower than men's owing to the persistent gender wage gap, and that women migrant workers may also pay up to 20 percent more in remittance transfer fees than men. For example, more Ukrainian women migrate for work to the European Union than men, and short-term women migrant workers remit more than men (€2,000 compared to €1,806), even though they tend to earn less money while abroad.[1] Migrant women face multiple and intersecting forms of discrimination, not only as women and as migrants but also on the basis of interconnected characteristics such as age, ethnicity, religion, marital and family status, and disability. This discrimination and the lack of basic employment rights for migrant workers exacerbates their vulnerability to abuse at work, including trafficking, forced labor, and economic violence such as withholding of pay and under- or nonpayment.

For example, paid domestic work is a very important and expanding source of wage employment for migrant women. The majority of this work is informal, arduous, and of poor quality. As of 2010, the overwhelming majority (83 percent) of the 53 million domestic workers in the world were women, and nearly 12 million girls aged 5–17 were in paid domestic work.[2] Domestic workers carry out their duties in the private homes of their employers, with whom they have a subordinate and dependent relationship. Psychological and physical abuse by the employer or family members is extremely prevalent and can occur with impunity given that national labor laws in both sending and receiving countries often exclude migrant workers (such as in the majority of countries in the Middle East and North Africa, where migrant work is widespread).

Aside from poor legal protections, migrant domestic workers are particularly vulnerable to abuse due to their dependence on recruitment agencies and lack of reliable information on migration procedures. In many national jurisdictions, they have limited freedom to change employers, and leaving their employer may mean leaving the country. If they attempt to flee their abusive employers, migrant domestic workers often face further victimization. Specifically, some employers maliciously file absconding reports or submit false claims of theft or other crimes. As a result, workers can face administrative and criminal fines, imprisonment, deportation, and bans on re-entering the country. A 2014 Human Rights Watch report on female migrant domestic workers in the United Arab

Emirates (UAE) found that it was common for fleeing migrant domestic workers to have absconding charges brought against them because of a 2007 law that incentivized employers to report absent domestic workers. This encouraged employers in the UAE to monitor and restrict domestic workers' freedom of movement. Likewise, a 2016 Human Rights Watch report on the same situation in Oman cited several incidents wherein women domestic workers experiencing abuse sought help at hospitals and police stations, only to be imprisoned and/or returned to their employers, where they experienced significant further violence.

What forms of VAWG do migrant women and girls experience on the migration journey?

Traveling along certain migration corridors poses significant risks for women and girls. This includes, but is not limited to, the risk of physical or sexual violence by criminal groups, human traffickers, corrupt border agents, and other migrants. For example, the UN estimates that 60 to 80 percent of migrant women and girls traveling through Mexico to the United States are raped at some stage during their transit. In fact, in 2018 a *New York Times* article revealed the frightening experiences of abuse that women crossing the US-Mexico border face from border patrol agents and customs officers. In one case, a 14-year-old girl traveling with a friend and the friend's mother from Honduras was taken by a border patrol agent to an isolated area, where they were sexually assaulted. Likewise, UN estimates show that along the central Mediterranean route, up to 90 percent of women and girls are raped traveling to Italy. While migrant women may seek to protect themselves from violence during their journey by traveling with a male partner or relative, these companions may also be responsible for the perpetration of violence against women.

Many migrant women and girls rely on smugglers to help them cross borders and move through countries, often leaving them in debt under exploitative pay-as-you-go arrangements and more vulnerable to sexual abuse, economic exploitation, and trafficking. Desperation and poverty may force migrant women and girls into survival sex—for example, providing sex as an alternative form of payment in return for their passage. The UN Office for Drugs and Crime (UNODC) reported that in one case of migration from West Africa to Norway, criminal actors offered migrant women an irregular migration package, including transportation and counterfeit documents, for roughly €250. One woman accepted this offer with the intention of paying the fee upon arrival in Europe; however, when she reached Norway, the traffickers raised the debt to €50,000 and forced her to repay it through forced street prostitution.[3] This is a form of economic as well as physical and sexual VAWG, since controlling women's use of resources, denying women access to funds, and preventing women from gaining legal employment are all part of the international definition of VAWG.

We know that VAWG is deeply connected to the unequal division of power and resources between men and women. This division is greatly exacerbated during migration, because migration agents and recruiters, foreign employers, traveling partners and children, and other migrants all contribute to these power relationships. As expressed by ILO chief technical adviser Deepa Bharathi in 2018, "If not reined in by gender-equitable and migrant-equitable labor laws, none of these actors have a reason, beyond their own ethics, to ensure women migrant workers receive due pay, fair recruitment procedures, and decent working conditions able to prevent violence and abuse."[4]

A pertinent example arises from ongoing mass migration occurring across the borders of Myanmar and Thailand. Myanmar's prolonged humanitarian crisis over the last 40 years has led to significant migration of men and women to Thailand and via Thailand to other destinations. Of an estimated 3.25 million labor migrants in Thailand, the majority are

from Myanmar. Due to an overwhelming lack of legal migration documentation, most migrants occupy low-cost and undocumented labor positions, making them vulnerable to abuse
and exploitation. On the Thai-Myanmar border, a 2019 study
of over 500 migrant workers found that women faced pervasive sexual violence during transit, and that female migrants
were at significant risk of various forms of sexual violence and
abuse, both during their migration journey and once established in workplaces.[5]

How is access to justice for women migrants experiencing VAWG being addressed?

Both international and state responses are necessary to prevent
and respond to violence against migrant women and girls. For
example, Nepal's Foreign Employment Act, adopted by the
government in 2008, ensures equal opportunities for women
and men working abroad and socioeconomic protection for
migrant workers and their families. The Nepalese government
has also provided shelters for returned migrants both in Nepal
and in other major destinations for Nepali women workers
(Kuwait, UAE, Saudi Arabia, and Qatar) to support rescue
and repatriation. The Nepalese government regulates how domestic workers are recruited and placed in several countries.
Nepalese diplomatic missions ensure that foreign employment agencies are legitimate. In the Philippines, the amended
Migrant Workers and Overseas Filipinos Act strengthens the
protections for overseas nationals by ensuring that they only
work in countries that protect migrant workers' rights and welfare, particularly those of women migrant domestic workers.
Finally, in Sri Lanka, measures introduced by the Sri Lanka
Bureau of Foreign Employment have resulted in a ban on
migrating for work overseas for prospective women domestic
workers with children under the age of five years. While initially introduced in response to the execution of a Sri Lankan
domestic worker in Saudi Arabia in 2013, its roots are in fact

more gendered, with the government and courts affirming that the ban was put in place to ensure that women remained primary caregivers in their families. This has sparked significant controversy in Sri Lanka and claims of gender discrimination, with concerns that the measure increases women's vulnerability to trafficking since women will now likely seek illegal opportunities to work abroad through trafficking networks.

Given that state solutions are limited in their capacity to eliminate violence against migrant women and girls, strong regional responses are needed. There has been some progress in Southeast Asia. Specifically, in 2017 the Association of Southeast Asian Nations (ASEAN) established a consensus framework on the Protection and Promotion of the Rights of Migrant Workers. This nonbinding consensus provides general principles on the fundamental rights of migrant workers (particularly women and their family members), as well as the obligations and commitments of ASEAN member states. It aims to improve cooperation among ASEAN states with regard to regional issues that migrant workers face, including VAWG. We can see this embodied in the EU and UN's Spotlight Initiative to ensure that labor migration is safe and fair for all women in the ASEAN region, otherwise known as the Safe & Fair program. This program confronts women migrant workers' vulnerabilities to violence by improving the frameworks that govern labor migration and VAWG, increasing access to information and services for women migrant workers, and building up a knowledge base of the experiences of women migrant workers to understand their contribution and better inform campaigns to improve their situation.

Several international conventions extend protections to migrant women and girls. As discussed in chapter 10, the ILO's Convention 190 on Violence and Harassment (adopted in 2019) is the first international standard specifically addressing violence and harassment in the world of work. Alongside detailed workplace protections, the Convention recognizes that vulnerable groups, such as migrants, may be disproportionately affected by violence and harassment at work, and it calls for states to ensure the right to equality and nondiscrimination in employment and occupation. Furthermore, ILO Convention 189 on Domestic Workers, which became effective in 2013, aims to secure the rights and protection of domestic workers worldwide, the vast majority of whom are women and/or migrants. This Convention requires states to grant the same rights to domestic workers as other workers, including normal work hours and rest periods, overtime compensation, minimum wage guarantees, and annual paid leave. Unfortunately, this Convention is one of the least ratified, with just 29 countries having ratified it as of the end of 2019. In his report on violence against women migrant workers in 2019, the UN Secretary-General noted that the number of states ratifying international instruments relevant to tackling violence and discrimination against women migrant workers has only marginally increased since 2017, representing a significant issue for international efforts to eliminate VAWG.

What is human trafficking, and how is it a form of VAWG? How pervasive is trafficking globally?

Human trafficking is a form of forced migration. It is big business worth an estimated US$150 billion annually and, according to UNODC, 10 percent world total GDP.[6] The UN Protocol to Prevent, Suppress and Punish Trafficking in Persons defines human trafficking as "the recruitment, transportation, transfer, harboring or receipt of persons, by means of the threat or use of force or other forms of coercion, of abduction, of fraud, of deception, of the abuse of power or of a position of vulnerability or of the giving or receiving of payments or benefits to achieve the consent of a person having control over another person, for the purpose of exploitation."[7]

Estimates by the ILO suggest that globally, 40.3 million people have been trafficked, predominantly for forced labor and sexual exploitation. This trafficking inevitably occurs in a gendered way: the largest share is for sexual exploitation, and of those trafficked for sex, 96 percent are women and girls; conversely, of those trafficked for forced labor, 63 percent are men. In this sense, trafficking disproportionately affects women and girls and is therefore a significant form of VAWG. It should be noted, however, that women and girls are also trafficked for reasons other than sexual exploitation, although that is far less common. According to the UN Secretary-General's report on trafficking in women and girls, women and girls may also be trafficked for forced labor, forced marriages, begging, and domestic servitude.

Trafficking remains a major global challenge. High-income countries in western and southern Europe, the Middle East, and North America are the main trafficking destinations. The largest trafficking flows originate from eastern Europe, Central Asia, South America, and South Asia. Those from sub-Saharan Africa and East Asia are more globally dispersed. Ultimately, the majority of victims are trafficked transnationally (across country borders), with the remainder trafficked domestically.

As global inequalities grow, they push the poorest people (particularly women) to seek out better economic opportunities in wealthier countries, which increases their vulnerability to trafficking. At the same time, low-income countries possess fewer resources for sustainable development and less capital to invest in services and infrastructure to reduce poverty, thus further contributing to the trafficking of women and girls.

Research has shown that sex trafficking accelerates particularly in regions facing natural disasters or insecurity, including climate-fueled disasters and armed conflicts. These events increase economic instability and strain health and other services, which in turn increases the risk of trafficking for women and girls. This is particularly relevant where women and girls become separated from their families, or where families resort to trafficking to earn money because normal income channels have been destroyed.

Migration policies can also exacerbate vulnerabilities to trafficking for women and girls as the lack of sufficient accessible, legal pathways for migration forces people to pursue riskier route and transport options. Even though restrictive migration policies are often introduced to prevent trafficking, the lack of viable pathways for people to migrate for economic opportunities actually increases their risk of being trafficked.

Migrant women's and girls' vulnerability to violence and trafficking is inextricable from their unequal economic and social status. Globally, women and girls are overrepresented among the poor: according to the UN Secretary-General's 2018 report, there are over 330 million women and girls living on less than US$1.90 per day, with 4.4 million more women living at this level than men. Given women's propensity to occupy precarious jobs, poverty and lack of decent work opportunities may push women to migrate or seek risky employment situations in which they may be coerced, abused, or trafficked. Likewise, efforts to escape violent situations may inevitably lead women and girls to make dangerous choices that place them at heightened risk of trafficking.

12

VAWG AND
LAND/PROPERTY RIGHTS

*Are women and girls without legal equality in rights
to land, property, inheritance, access to credit, and
business ownership more vulnerable to VAWG?*

Land and property rights provide a structural context through which gendered power is reorganized, increasing women's empowerment and making them less vulnerable to violence and abuse. The possession of land and property rights ensures basic human rights to shelter and livelihood, which are recognized sources of wealth, power, and social status. Furthermore, land and the capital it can generate give financial security to women and improve their bargaining power vis-à-vis men in the household and at the community level, providing expanded social status and increasing women's sense of individual agency and self-efficacy. This enhanced status and power may reduce overall gender discrimination, including the risk of VAWG, by giving women more control over decisions that affect their lives.

For example, research by Grabe, Grose, and Dutt (2015) found that when rural women in Nicaragua and Tanzania own land, they gain power and status within their communities, leading to greater control within their relationships and lowered experiences of violence. Specifically, property ownership interrupted patriarchal sociocultural structures by strengthening women's ability to independently address their needs; several women explained how reductions in violence ensued from their decreased dependence on their husbands. Likewise, Bina Agarwal and Pradeep Panda found that in India, the risk of domestic violence against women was 50 percent less when a woman owned property, either her own home or land.[1] In this sense, women's ownership of land and property can act as a major deterrent to violence against them, leveling the playing field with men and allowing women to protect and depend upon themselves. The converse is also true: a lack of land and property rights or the absence or removal of those rights can increase the risk women face of VAWG. For instance, Song and Dong (2017) investigated the relationship between women's land rights status and their risk of violence in rural China following several agricultural reforms that increased women's landlessness due to patrilocal and patrilineal customs. They found that both the loss of claim to contract land and having no residential land in a woman's own name increased a woman's probability of experiencing physical violence, psychological violence, and any type of domestic violence.

Importantly, women's having land rights and property ownership can have a beneficial impact on VAWG at both the individual and community level. Responding to this potential relationship between land rights and reduced VAWG, a community-level intervention in western Kenya was designed to respond to violations of women's property rights in order to reduce VAWG. Specifically, the community program enabled women to report property rights violations and receive assistance concerning land disputes, property grabbing (large-scale land acquisitions by private investors), and instances of disinheritance and unfair eviction. It also facilitated community education and discussion around women's rights and VAWG. The study found that nearly all women who reported property rights violations and violence during disinheritance also reported that violence at the individual level stopped immediately. In addition, the program resulted in a reduction of sexual and domestic VAWG at the community level due to improved knowledge about women's rights and VAWG, the existence of a responsive reporting mechanism, and perpetrator fears about legal consequences.

However, it is important to remember that the relationship between VAWG and land/property rights is complex and dependent on local norms and structures. For instance, Vyas and colleagues (2015) studied urban women market traders in Tanzania and found in one district that the women who earned money and who owned a business suffered from a higher risk of intimate partner violence. There are also other studies that suggest there is either a negative or simply no correlation between women's increased ownership of land/property and VAWG.[2] One explanation for this opposite trend is that women who gain higher bargaining power through their access to economic resources challenge male authority and their conception of being the sole provider, leading to greater violence and backlash against women's improved economic position. However, despite the few findings associated with this view, the majority of current research suggests a positive relationship between women's land and property ownership and reduced VAWG.

Women's property or home ownership also provides clear advantages in helping them deal with domestic violence situations by providing economic security. A majority of women surveyed in the Tanzanian study reported that ownership of property could prevent marital conflict and was also a protection in case of such conflict. Among propertied women who experienced violence, the majority indicated that they attempted to change the situation within their relationship; on the other hand, nonpropertied women experiencing violence highlighted that the lack of ownership of property meant they could not walk out of an abusive relationship. In this sense, the critical advantage of property was economic; property acted as a form of protection in times of economic crisis, old age, and widowhood, as well as a type of insurance and option for income generation.

Is VAWG perpetrated to expropriate land, natural resources, and other valuable material assets?

Violence against women and girls has been strategically used by both states and nonstate actors to forcibly move communities off resource-rich land. The UN Secretary-General's report on conflict-related sexual violence in 2018 confirmed that sexual violence has been perpetrated against women and girls in order to displace communities, expel undesirable groups and seize control or gain access to contested land and other resources.[3] Importantly, resource-rich areas are attractive not only to military, rebels, and militia groups, but also to police, public agents, and businesses, all of whom might adopt various tactics for controlling the land and gaining access to riches. In particular, parties to a conflict may operate in poorly controlled areas with massive potential economic gains as a means to finance warfare and therefore may use VAWG to ensure ongoing access to and control over valuable natural resources.

In eastern Democratic Republic of the Congo (DRC), for instance, it is well-documented that rape has been strategically used by armed actors to drive out settled populations in order to gain access to land and valuable resources. Sexual violence may be used as a tool of domination to subjugate and terrorize the civilian population, enabling access to and control over a region's mines and vast mineral wealth. The majority of armed actors profit from the extortion of the civilian population and the extraction of natural resources that can be performed using basic technology, both of which prolong violence and instability.

Violence and intimidation also continue to be perpetrated within the context of armed conflict in Colombia to forcefully displace populations from lucrative mining or agricultural areas and in corridors that are strategic for drug trafficking. For instance, a 2011 report submitted to the US Committee on Foreign Affairs suggested that guerrilla groups and organized criminal groups were responsible for preventing food and medicine delivery to towns that lay across contested drug-trafficking corridors in Colombia as a means to weaken their economies and deplete their resources, thereby increasing forced displacement.[4] The displacement of communities contributes to a general state of lawlessness, weakening traditional mechanisms for social control and order. Communities that are characterized by a lack of social control tend to see higher levels of sexual violence and an increase in overall VAWG.

In another context, the expropriation of land for large infrastructure projects can lead to increased VAWG. For example, long-term building and development schemes, such as those supported by the World Bank and other international donors, may involve a substantial influx of male migrant workers into otherwise rural and isolated communities. This intrusion can expose women and girls to heightened risk of sexual exploitation and abuse, especially given the unequal power and resources between rural women and migrant men, as was the case with the gender-based violence perpetrated in the context of the World Bank–funded Uganda Transport Sector Development Project in December 2015. As a result, the World Bank and other institutions now apply standards for gender-based violence risk identification, mitigation, and response to all new operations in sustainable development and infrastructure sectors. For instance, new projects by the World Bank involve (among other things) a worker code of conduct, a grievance redress mechanism with a specific mandate to address gender-based violence, and concrete survivor-centered measures to empower women and to bolster their economic opportunities during projects.

What is the impact of resource extraction industries on VAWG?

Resource extraction industries have a significant impact on the risk factors and overall prevalence of VAWG. Resource extraction frequently occurs in precarious environments and in rural settings, where conflict, population influx, lack of resource access, limited education, and poor healthcare can compound vulnerabilities to VAWG. In the context of resource extraction, a new category of violence is emerging, which Doris Buss refers to as "conflict mining-related sexual violence."[5] Though still in its early stages of recognition and research, this type of VAWG is defined by the collection of sexual violence data in the context of resource extraction during seemingly intractable conflicts.

There are economic incentives to continue conflict in resource-rich areas, and both strategic and opportunistic VAWG may be perpetrated by police and security personnel. Armed actors who rely heavily on natural resources to fund their war activities are particularly likely to include individuals who will opportunistically commit significant abuses against civilian populations. Violence against women and girls may also be used to move populations away from land and resources where mining is taking place. For example, in Colombia soldiers have been brought in to protect mega mining projects, and proximate to these areas there has been a notable increase in violence and conflict. ABColombia (a consortium of five UK and Irish NGOs working on human rights and development in Colombia) found that increased military presence has led to an increase in human rights violations especially involving women, such as prostitution of indigenous girls and women, unwanted pregnancy, and sexual violence.[6] In this sense, there is a strong interaction between violence perpetrated in the context of natural resource extraction and conflict-related VAWG, as discussed in chapter 5.

Artisanal and small-scale mining (ASM), a basic yet labor-intensive form of mining that provides an important livelihood to swathes of people in Africa and South Asia, is another area of resource extraction involving VAWG. Examining the connection between ASM and sexual violence in eastern DRC, Rustad, Østby, and Nordås assessed survey data on the geographical location of mine sites and women's exposure to

sexual violence.[7] They found that women living in close prox-
imity to mine sites were more likely to experience sexual violence, especially nonpartner sexual violence. At the same time,
the lack of knowledge regarding women's right to safe and fair
work in mines in the DRC has led some women to use sex as a
transactional act to acquire protection and marginal economic
gains while working. Notably, male artisanal miners are not
the sole perpetrators of VAWG in and around ASM areas; the
presence of police and army officials in ASM zones has also
been found to contribute to increased insecurity for women.
Unfortunately, cases of abuse are rarely reported to the authorities, and even more rarely do they make it through the judicial system, creating a culture of impunity around this type
of VAWG.

Both ASM and large-scale mining have been found to have
myriad negative impacts on local communities. First, when
land is sold to or occupied by mining companies, rural communities lose access to communal and common land previously used for subsistence agriculture, for which women are
primarily responsible. This loss of access to livelihood activities heavily affects women in terms of coping with decreasing
food security, while simultaneously increasing their vulnerability to precarious forms of income generation, including
transactional sex, bonded labor, and trafficking.

Women are disproportionately affected by many of the negative impacts of mining. Health consequences stem from the
dangerous roles women undertake in the sector. Specifically,
inadequate attention to health and safety and the physically
demanding nature of tasks commonly undertaken by women
can result in chronic injury, lung fibrosis, and harmful exposure to toxic substances. These negative impacts decrease
women's security and ability to generate income and resources
and increase their risk of violence.

Resource extraction industries also affect women's livelihoods on several levels, many of which operate as forms of
economic violence. For example, in South Asian countries,

when a woman marries a bonded laborer (someone who is forced to work to pay off a debt and the value of whose labor is often greater than the debt), she simultaneously marries the conditions of his bondage. Critically, this arrangement can result in intergenerational bondage, including child bondage. Where this occurs, for instance in the case of a woman head of a household being in bondage following her husband's death, the consequences include forced work for extreme hours and often outside of usual jobs, as well as total disempowerment because of the inability to control the arrangement, which inevitably increases her vulnerability to abuse.

Part 3

CONTEXTS AND IMPACTS

13

EDUCATION, SCHOOLS, AND VAWG

How is VAWG perpetrated at school and through educational processes and curricula?

School-related gender-based violence (SRGBV) and VAWG occurring within the context of educational institutions are problems in all countries in the world and cut across cultural, geographic, and economic differences in societies. They can be defined as acts or threats of violence occurring in and around schools, perpetrated as a result of gender norms and stereotypes, and enforced by unequal power dynamics due to age and gender between and among teachers and students. The VAWG within schools includes physical, verbal, psychological, emotional, and sexual violence, as well as the fear or threat of violence and bullying.

While there is a lack of global comparable data on the various forms of VAWG in schools or educational institutions, many agencies, governments, and researchers have collected data on SRGBV. Overall, the UN estimates that 246 million children and adolescents experience school violence and bullying in some form every year. For instance, Plan International's 2013 report on SRGBV collated data across global regions and national studies. It found that sexual violence against schoolgirls appeared to be an institutional norm in several sub-Saharan African countries. Such violence included inappropriate sexual relations between male teachers and female students, transactional sex to cover school fees and the cost of school materials, sex for grades, and excessive use of corporal punishment. In Chile, Costa Rica, Panama, and Peru, national surveys[1] have found that 5–40 percent of adolescent girls had reported experiencing sexual abuse in a school context, and in the Dominican Republic, Honduras, Guatemala, Mexico, Panama, and Nicaragua, girls have reported experiences of sexual coercion from teachers under the threat of their grades suffering if they did not acquiesce. More egregiously, in Asia and the Pacific, girl students and teachers of girls have been killed, attacked, and threatened by armed groups whose ideologies oppose the education of girls, the education of girls of a certain age, or the education of girls alongside boys. In particular, Pakistan and Afghanistan are two countries in which girls' schooling and schools have been attacked, most commonly by being set on fire or bombed.

School-related gender-based violence operates by discriminating against specific groups whose education may lead them to oppose traditional gender and social norms, including women and girls, ethnic minorities, people living with disabilities, LGBTQI+ persons, and indigenous students. According to a 2016 UNESCO report, LGBT students report a higher prevalence of violence at school than their non-LGBT peers; similarly, in a survey of over 3,500 primary schoolchildren in Uganda, 24 percent of 11- to 14-year-old girls with disabilities reported sexual violence at school, compared to 12 percent of nondisabled girls.

Both teachers and students perpetrate school-related VAWG, which often includes sexual assault and harassment, bullying, and cyberbullying. Sexual harassment is one of the most common forms of VAWG committed by teachers against students. Though we expect teachers to prevent violence at school, those in positions of power can be perpetrators of sexual abuse and exploitation, often acting with impunity. A 2010 survey by the Ministry of National Education in Côte d'Ivoire, for example, found that 47 percent of teachers reported having elicited sexual relations with their students.[2] On university campuses, too, there are high rates of sexual harassment and assault globally. For example, a survey conducted in 2019 by the Association of American Universities (AAU) engaged with 181,000 students across 33 participating institutions to discuss sexual assault and misconduct on campus. It found that 26 percent of female undergraduates had experienced non-consensual contact through physical force or because they were unable to give consent, while 59 percent had experienced harassing behavior. Likewise, an Australian Human Rights Commission survey in 2017 of over 30,000 students at 39 institutions found that one in five students had been sexually harassed in a university setting, and that postgraduate students were almost twice as likely as undergraduate students to have been sexually harassed by a lecturer or tutor from their university.

Bullying and cyberbullying comprise another widely documented type of violence affecting women and girls in schools. A US study in 2012 of more than 20,000 high school students found a substantial overlap between school bullying and cyberbullying.[3] Notably, girls were more likely than boys to report being victims of cyberbullying in combination with school bullying (11 percent compared to 8 percent). Furthermore, 23 percent of nonheterosexual students reported being victims of both cyberbullying and school bullying, compared to only 9 percent of students who identified as heterosexual. Bullying is frequently expressed through gendered power relations, and students may become targets for bullies if they choose not to conform to expected gender norms or their real or perceived gender identity. Interestingly, studies[4] in Australia, the United States, and Latin America found boys to be more involved in physical and verbal bullying (both as perpetrators or victims), whereas girls were found to be more prone to psychological forms of bullying, such as social ostracization and rumor spreading.

The rise of the internet and use of text messages, email, and social media on smartphones has enabled new forms of violence among schoolchildren and young people. The most available data on the prevalence of cyberbullying is from surveys conducted in industrialized countries and suggests that up to 20 percent of children and adolescents are likely to experience cyberbullying, with girls more susceptible to abuse than boys.[5] This risk appears to translate into young adulthood, with women university students particularly vulnerable to attack through cyberbullying such as non-consensual sexting, morphing, virtual rape, and revenge porn.

Corporal punishment is another form of SRGBV. While on the decline in developed countries, it is estimated that over half of all children worldwide live in countries where they are not legally protected from corporal punishment in schools, 45 percent living in South Asia alone.[6] The performance of corporal punishment is gendered: studies show that some male teachers use physical punishment to assert their authority, particularly against boys perceived as tough and undisciplined, whereas female teachers may be more likely to use verbal chastisement, and girls are more often punished for not being sufficiently submissive and ladylike in the classroom.

What is the role of educational institutions and systems in preventing VAWG?

Schools and educational institutions are uniquely positioned to prevent VAWG. There is a need for both a coordinated, multifaceted approach to tackle violence in schools and universities and recognition of the relationship between different forms of violence occurring within and outside the educational environment.

Schools can provide gender-sensitive education to students and teachers that promotes healthy and respectful relationships, gender equality, and health education to prevent unwanted and unsafe sex. Curricula that integrate discussions of gender issues, including gender-based violence, rights, and power dynamics, can be particularly effective in empowering girls. For example, male and female secondary school and university students who have attended rape education sessions show less adherence to rape myths, express fewer rape-supportive attitudes, and report greater victim empathy than those who have not attended. Likewise, programs promoting nonviolence among men and boys and positive masculinities through nonviolent male role models have demonstrated positive shifts in attitudes toward VAWG. The Tomorrow Man program in Australia, for instance, is an intensive program allowing teenage boys to explore what it means to be a man and to increase their emotional capacity and expression. Its programming seeks to disrupt men's anger and its violent expressions that are socialized in traditional Western forms of masculinity, thereby helping to revise the gender norms that underpin VAWG.

Ensuring a safe school environment that has appropriate physical facilities, including school buildings, grounds, water and sanitation facilities, furniture, lighting, and security equipment, is also important for the prevention of school-related VAWG. This is because VAWG in schools and educational institutions is exacerbated by poorly designed or managed infrastructure, such as dim lighting or broken locks, as well as physical isolation and inadequate supervision of facilities where girls are active. One means of remedying this risk factor is through participatory mapping, which was used in a USAID-funded project in the DRC to identify places where schoolgirls felt unsafe in and around school.[7] Through consultations and design revisions, this mapping helped to inform school communities where to prioritize infrastructure funding to lower the risk of VAWG in and around school.

Furthermore, clear and effective codes of conduct in schools and educational institutions for teachers and students can prevent and dissuade violence or abuse. In particular, these codes should prohibit all forms of violence and provide effective procedures for reporting and monitoring incidents of SRGBV. For instance, the Safe Schools Program in Malawi, which adopted a revised Teachers' Code of Conduct, significantly increased the number of teachers who were aware of how to report violations and their sense of responsibility to do so. Safe and accessible reporting procedures and mechanisms are important in terms of addressing SRGBV so that students can report violence and abuse free from intimidation, while also knowing that there will be services in place to support them. Reporting mechanisms can involve telephone helplines, chat rooms and online reporting, and "happiness and sadness" boxes, as well as school-based focal points, such as teachers or student counselors. For example, in 2008 a 24-hour telephone and web-based helpline was set up for children in Kenya, through which trained volunteer counselors provided support and referral services for children concerned about sexual, physical, and emotional abuse and neglect.[8] Through the introduction of this resource, girls frequently reported to the helpline that they had been sexually abused by their teachers, leading to over 1,000 teachers being removed from their jobs between 2009 and 2010.

The provision of counseling, support, and appropriate referral structures is also a responsibility of schools and educational institutions in order to prevent incidence and recurrence of VAWG. Support should be provided to victims of violence as well as to witnesses and perpetrators, especially students but also teachers. Referral structures ensure that victims of violence in schools and universities are guided to the services they require, such as medical treatment; law enforcement; child protection; emotional support; and other relevant health, behavioral, and legal services.

Finally, more broadly, schools and educational institutions that pursue positive gender-inclusive education practices can help inform the wider community and change communal knowledge regarding VAWG. Students are ambassadors in their communities and can share knowledge gained at school or university about the problem of gender-based VAWG, thereby promoting a cultural change toward a safer, more inclusive society.

How can educational programs increase awareness of VAWG and promote societal and behavioral change?

The curriculum is a crucial component in the prevention of VAWG and promotion of gender equality as a foundation for nonviolence. Education that encourages young people to question, negotiate, and challenge violence and gender discrimination is critical for preventing violence, including violence at school. Young people need to be able to recognize what constitutes violence and abuse, know how to protect themselves from harm, and take action to avoid harming others. Young people also need to be given the opportunity to develop positive notions of masculinities and femininities and an increased understanding and acceptance of sexual and gender diversity throughout society. There are several different curriculum entry points for children of all school-going ages to prevent violence and promote gender equality, including through comprehensive sexuality education (CSE), life skills education, civics education, targeted approaches on managing aggression, bystander skill development, healthy relationships classes, and bullying protection sessions. These programs are often most effective in combination.

Fortunately, there are myriad examples of positive gender education programs being adopted in curricula to help tackle VAWG throughout the world. In Uganda, CSE aims to equip young people with knowledge, skills, and values about relationships, gender, sexuality, and violence so that they can make informed and healthy choices. The World Starts with Me is a low-tech, online, interactive sex education program aimed at students aged 12–19. It uses virtual peer educators to guide students through 14 lessons and assignments in self-esteem, healthy relationships, sexual development, safe sex, gender equality, and sexual rights. Likewise, in India the Gender Equity Movement in Schools (GEMS) project was implemented in public schools using extracurricular activities, role-playing, and games with boys and girls aged 12–14. An evaluation of the program's effectiveness in 80 schools in Jharkhand found a positive and significant shift in attitudes toward gender and violence among students in GEMS schools, as well as a decline in acceptance of violence among peers, improved communication between students (including between boys and girls), enhanced recognition of violence and bystander intervention, and changes in reported perpetration of violence.[9]

Educational programs related to VAWG are also important in higher education. In Australia, following a 2017 Human Rights Commission report on sexual assault and harassment in universities, Monash University developed a campaign to promote its Respectful & Responsible module, in which all students were automatically enrolled and some students were required to complete (if, for instance, they were student leaders or attending an off-campus event). The module seeks to foster healthy and mutually respectful relationships, encourage safe bystander intervention, and promote changes in attitudes and social norms to create a safer, more inclusive university community. Moreover, a sexual assault resistance program has been established for first-year female university students. It consists of four three-hour units involving games, lectures, discussion, and application and practice activities designed to empower women to trust their judgment and overcome social pressures to be polite or friendly when they feel their bodily integrity being threatened.

Furthermore, school-based clubs and other types of safe spaces can be a useful entry point for addressing school-related VAWG. Most interventions in this area so far have engaged girls separately from boys, giving them their own space to speak freely; gain confidence; and improve their knowledge, attitudes, and practices in managing violence and inequality. For example, the Stop Violence Against Girls in School (SVAGS) school-based girls' clubs in Ghana, Kenya, and Mozambique allow girls to meet, discuss issues, and support each other throughout adolescence.[10] Specifically, these clubs use debates, theater, camps, and visits to other communities as a way to educate members on violence and carry out anti-VAWG advocacy. In fact, girls in clubs in Mozambique were found to be almost twice as likely to report violence as girls not in clubs, demonstrating the impact of the clubs on improving girls' knowledge, attitudes, and confidence in challenging VAWG.

That being said, boys' clubs are also a valuable resource in gender education. Another example of an extracurricular approach to anti-VAWG education is school-based cricket clubs for boys in India. These clubs train cricket coaches and community leaders to address issues of gender-based violence by raising awareness about abusive behavior, promoting gender-equitable and nonviolent attitudes, and teaching skills to speak up when witnessing harmful and disrespectful behavior toward women. Evaluation studies found positive changes in the cricket players' attitudes to VAWG, as well as some decline in their level of peer violence.[11]

Finally, pedagogy and teacher training are also extremely important for VAWG prevention, as what children learn and how it is taught are fundamental to their experiences in school. To tackle violence in and around schools, teachers need to be more aware of the various dynamics in their classrooms, including those of gender, power, race, ethnicity, and ability. Similarly, teachers need to also be more aware of their own biases and behaviors. Ideally, teachers should adopt equitable pedagogy, in which girls and boys receive the same treatment and attention, follow the same curriculum, and enjoy teaching methods and tools free of stereotypes and gender biases, thereby embracing difference and diversity in the classroom.

14

VAWG AND THE ENVIRONMENT

How are environmental changes related to VAWG?

Environmental changes that cause resource scarcity exacerbate VAWG. In societies where harmful traditional practices continue to regard women as property, resource scarcities intensify gender-based VAWG. Moreover, extreme weather events can exacerbate insecurities and foreshadow gender-based violence. For example, in pastoralist societies in Kenya where extreme weather has led to extreme drought, women and girls have experienced forced or child marriages at an even younger age. This gives their families access to cattle, which are exchanged upon marriage and on which people rely to survive. Increases in another form of VAWG, FGM/C, as discussed in detail in chapter 7, have also occurred as families prepare girls for early marriage across tribal groups to provide income and mitigate losses from agriculture due to drought (see Tanyag and True 2019).

Being at high risk and having a low capacity to respond to environmental changes in some countries are compounded by gender inequalities. Women and girls constitute a majority of displaced populations globally that suffer human rights violations, including VAWG, due to environmental change. This is because environmental change and disasters resulting from it discriminate against groups with lesser capacities, resources, and opportunities, including minorities, disabled persons, women, and girls. Primarily, disasters have a greater effect on women's mortality than men's; the disproportionate figure of 70 percent female deaths and women being a large proportion of displaced persons as a result of the Indian Ocean Asian tsunami in 2004 are illustrative of this gender inequality and gender-based VAWG, as also revealed by analysis of the 2010 floods in Pakistan.[1] Survival strategies in the aftermath of environmental disasters, such as marrying off daughters to generate income in the context of debt and dependency on humanitarian assistance, further reinforce the gender inequalities that partly produced the initial displacement.

Environmental changes can also result in changes to economic situations that exacerbate VAWG. Economic systems based on free market economics and neoliberalism tend to disadvantage women, whose economic activity is disproportionately in the nonmarket sphere. Women comprise the majority of those living in poverty and are made vulnerable by pregnancy, workplace discrimination, economic inequality, domestic violence, and—underpinning all else—socially constructed caring roles. When environmental disasters occur, their consequences include a disproportionate loss of employment for women, more women in precarious economic situations, wage decreases felt more significantly by women than men, higher levels of stress-related illnesses, and increased male VAWG.

Importantly, environmental changes affecting women's economic situations produce problems in both developed and developing countries. In Australia, for instance, in the context of environmental changes affecting rural women and farm incomes, rural women have been found to take on extra paid work to address the loss of income for a family in situations of drought, flooding, and bushfires. According to the Australian Women's Health Network, approximately 37 percent of farm income comes from off-farm employment, and 73 percent of women have needed to seek off-farm work in the context of environmental disaster.[2] Throughout Australia, men's reactions to the stress associated with this loss of income and the challenge to their traditional breadwinner roles has often been violent and may represent an attempt to reclaim some level of power and control after a disaster. More broadly, environmental disaster has intensified the everyday justification and acceptance of men's violence in Australia. Empathy for men who perpetrate domestic violence but are "good blokes" and heroes during natural disasters, for example, results in the silencing of women and dismissal of their experiences of violence, especially when the men appear to be suffering or suicidal. The experience of disaster may also be seen as reason enough for losing control and behaving violently, and men's violence is rarely censured in male-dominated cultures in emergency or community organizations.

Why is there an increase in VAWG during and after natural disasters?

The major reason women and girls are particularly vulnerable to violence during and after natural disasters is in fact their economic and social status *before* disaster strikes. Women are generally poorer than men, do not own land or have property rights, are less likely to have an education or access to healthcare, and have less of a political voice in environmental planning and decision-making. Likewise, the impact of an environmental disaster depends on the overall human capabilities and resources of a society, which tends to magnify a society's divisions and inequalities. As pre-disaster gender inequalities increase, the number of women likely to be killed during and as a result of a disaster increases also. During and after disasters, women and girls are more vulnerable to death and violence due to socially constructed gender relations and preexisting patterns of gender inequality and discrimination. As disasters become frequent and more intense due to climate change, eliminating gender inequalities is vital to prevent VAWG.

Environmental disasters and the effects of climate change have been shown to intensify poverty in families and preexisting unequal gender norms, which has in turn determined the kind of stopgap coping measures and negative adaptations undertaken to survive. Many of these involve an increase in the risk and perpetration of VAWG. The 2004 Asian tsunami, which killed over 230,000 and resulted in significant injury and displacement, pertinently illustrates this relationship between disaster and gender-based inequality and violence.[3] Pervasive gender inequalities in education, literacy, income, land, political representation, and employment in coastal regions contributed to the disproportionate loss of female lives. Violence against women and girls increased significantly in the immediate aftermath, especially domestic violence, rape, sexual assault, and harassment. Young orphaned girls and women separated from their families were most vulnerable to violence. In the aftermath and recovery, compensation was given only to male heads of households and often not shared with women, leading to an increase in forced or early marriages as a means for poor families to provide for basic needs. The lack of adequate housing in post-tsunami camps further increased the incidence of sexual VAWG, and women who later became pregnant while unmarried or widowed were ostracized by their communities. Police and local authorities, mostly composed of men, were generally insensitive to the heightened vulnerability of women in the postdisaster context, meaning that women who felt the social stigma of rape or sexual assault did not feel comfortable coming forward. In fact, in some cases, policemen and paramilitaries were found to be the perpetrators of VAWG, generating further distrust and limiting women's access to justice.

What impact will climate change likely have on VAWG?

Climate change is not a gender-neutral phenomenon. Environmental disasters may be the product of, or intensified by, climate change and extreme weather, as shown in rising tides, typhoons, cyclones, flooding, wildfires, and droughts. Climate-induced extreme weather events are increasing in frequency and intensity, affecting many countries yet having an acute impact on the developing world. As these weather events increase and disasters result—indeed, as resource scarcity increases and conflicts result—we can expect VAWG to also increase.

As in disasters in general, women and girls are more vulnerable to death and violence in extreme climate-affected situations due to gender inequality and discrimination. Intensified demands on care provisioning to meet rising health and welfare needs have a greater impact on women than men, given that women are expected to care for others to the point of depleting their own health and well-being. A manifestation of climate change–related VAWG documented[4] in Malawi and Mozambique is that ever-younger girls are being married off by their families as an economic survival strategy. This practice produces a new generation of child brides, which in turn leads to dangerous early pregnancy and associated developmental complications for both mother and child. Furthermore, research in drought-prone areas in Bangladesh suggests that climate change is reinforcing dowry practices and forced or early marriages, as extreme drought intensifies economic pressures faced by poorer families.

Currently, climate-induced disasters are creating or contributing to mass displacement of populations, which adversely affects many women and girls. Specifically, the social dislocation and resettlement that come with the displacement of large populations may fuel instability and conflict. In such contexts, where some population groups are often marginalized or excluded, women and girls may become targets of abuse and exploitation. Climate change is a key trigger for forced or voluntary migration, which can bring short-term financial relief but can also lead to polygamy and other forms of gender-based violence and abuse. Research by Human Rights Watch (2015) shows how child marriage practices in Bangladesh are directly linked to climate-induced poverty. Similarly, in both Cambodia and Vietnam, climate change has been shown to be[5] a cause for mass migration and displacement, putting women at risk for trafficking or leaving them with the full responsibility to care for the family when men migrate—but without the same access to credit, land, or social resources as men.

Around the world, climate change–induced crises have also been shown to worsen VAWG, whether in relation to sexual and reproductive health or to discrimination against indigenous communities. For instance, the Asian-Pacific Resource and Research Centre for Women (ARROW) conducted a survey of 3,360 rural women from coastal communities and flood-prone or disaster-prone areas in 12 districts covering six divisions of Bangladesh.[6] It found that 93 percent of the shelters or emergency transitional homes were not women friendly, in the sense that they were not gender separated and inaccessible in their design, particularly for elderly and pregnant women. Furthermore, one-third of the respondents mentioned that sexual harassment takes place during disasters and in these shelters and transitional/emergency housing and, while largely perpetrated by strangers, included instances where male relatives were responsible for violence.

Climate change can aggravate conflict over resources and exacerbate VAWG. For many communities and regions in Africa and Asia, high resource dependence due to heavy reliance on agricultural production often produces competition over abundant or scarce resources, sometimes resulting in armed conflict. In these contexts, reports of human trafficking and gender-based violence increase, especially theft, physical abuse and assault, psychological abuse, sexual assault and harassment, reproductive violence linked to sexual violence (such as unwanted pregnancy, unsafe abortion, complications from high-risk pregnancy, and sexually transmitted disease), and exploitation (such as overpricing of goods and services). While many of these manifestations of violence are experienced by both men and women, most sexual harassment and assault is experienced by women.

How can we prevent VAWG through environmental planning and preparedness?

We can prevent VAWG in both situations of environmental change, disaster, and climate change and their aftermath. Two crucial strategies are promoting and enhancing women's political agency and resilience and integrating gender analysis of underlying inequalities and risk factors into early warning, preparedness, and recovery policies and programming. Often the low participation of women in planning and decision-making at the local, national, regional, and global levels acts as a barrier to effective responses to environmental disasters, resulting in insufficient attention being paid to gendered experiences of postdisaster violence.

In disaster contexts, women and girls are often depicted as vulnerable, weak, and dependent victims in need of protection, rather than as agents of community resilience and recovery. However, women's experience of environmental change, disaster, and recovery can lead them into collective action and leadership roles to shape new and sustainable solutions. For example, in Myanmar in 2010, responses to the effects of cyclone Nargis triggered and unified women's groups in civil society to address VAWG. Similarly, women's organizations across the Pacific Islands have come together to lead regional activism on climate change mitigation while also addressing gender-based violence in their communities. Initiatives such as FemLINKPacific's Women's Weather Watch, for instance, have mobilized women through community radio to negotiate risk reduction, adaptation strategies, alternative livelihoods, and community relocation.

Empowering women's community networks enables women to challenge men's dominance and the violence that prevents women from contributing their knowledge to environmental planning and preparedness policy processes, as well as from participating in timely crisis response. Women's community networks, such as Women I tok tok Tugeta (WITTT) in Vanuatu and the Tangulbei Women's Network (TAWN) in Kenya, allow groups of women to discuss their shared experiences and to advocate for their needs in formal government processes, including those in response to climate emergencies. By becoming part of the network, women are able to avoid the potential violence involved in individual activism, in which women may be singled out as threats to the community and targeted by men who wish to maintain their silence and exclusion.

Better governance and more participatory policymaking can prevent VAWG occurring both during and after environmental change and disasters. Analysis of gender inequalities and risks for violence should be mainstreamed into environmental assessments and disaster response strategies, while women's knowledge and leadership should inform all strategies and solutions for communities at risk of disaster and climate change. A range of new tools and indicators has emerged to enable this analysis, integrating country and subregional data on gender equality and women's empowerment, governance, livelihoods, and ecosystems. For example, the South Asia Women's Resilience Index (WRI) by ActionAid and the Economist Intelligence Unit measure preparedness for environmental and climate change across eight countries.[7] The WRI finds that seven out of eight countries have barely incorporated women's needs, such as protection from violence, in disaster responses or invested in women's capacities to prepare for disasters. The WRI shows that the lack of investment in gender equality in social, economic, infrastructural, and policy institutions renders countries highly vulnerable to disasters and magnifies the impacts of disasters and crises on women and girls, including VAWG. Overall, the WRI reveals areas where women's resilience for disaster risk reduction and recovery is poor. By monitoring and targeting these areas, it is possible to address gender inequalities in economic livelihoods and tackle high levels of violence against women as foundational issues that have an impact on environmental recovery. Policymakers and communities can also use indexes like the WRI to assess and prioritize areas for improving women's security as they prepare and plan responses to environmental and climate change–induced disasters.

15

INTERNATIONAL SECURITY AND VAWG

Why is VAWG a threat to international peace and security?

Gender-based violence against women, girls, men, boys, and gender-diverse groups invokes conflict and fuels acts of revenge, perpetuating cycles of violence. As conflicts flow over borders and/or draw in the militaries of other states in defense of territories and civilians, this violence threatens international peace and security. As mentioned in chapter 5 on conflict-related VAWG, this violence is not limited to acts of rape and sexual violence but incorporates increased intimate partner violence and an economy of gender-based violence, including enslavement, trafficking, forced or early marriage and pregnancy, detention and torture, kidnapping and forced disappearances (particularly of women activists and female members of male activists' families), denial of basic health services, and so on.

Most analytical frameworks for understanding conflict hold a very gendered view, taking men's experiences in the public realm to be the norm. As a result, research on international peace and security often fails to mention these types of violence or the gender dimensions of violence in general. In many contexts, VAWG is rendered invisible to the broader public by pervasive gendered stigmatization, which excludes meaningful acknowledgment of this violence and reinforces a culture of impunity. In particular, this stigmatization restricts women's access to the public sphere and limits men's alternatives to fighting. It is precisely this gendered stigmatization of VAWG, as well as sexualized violence against men and boys, that makes it an effective conflict tactic to politically repress populations and threaten international security. These tactics are effective in that gender norms compel women and men to keep silent about the violence they experience to prevent bringing dishonor to their families and communities.

Gender-based violence exploits stereotypes and reinforces oppression based on gender, ethnicity, class, caste, sexuality, or other identities. As such, gender-based violence may engender and/or exacerbate intergroup political violence and conflict. The symbolism and the stigma of gender-based violence can have a specific, catalytic effect on intrastate civil conflict, which has the potential to threaten international peace and security. To take an example from a current conflict: in Myanmar, Tatmadaw state military soldiers have immunity from civil prosecution and can therefore perpetrate VAWG with impunity, further fueling conflict with nonstate armed groups.[1] In this context and others, VAWG is not merely an embedded and permissive form of violence; rather, it serves as part of the dynamics of political violence. As the UN Secretary-General has argued in the UN Security Council,[2] sexual and gender-based violence have become a standard tool for controlling territory, dehumanizing victims, and recruiting new supporters. Failure to end impunity for this violence may therefore fuel broader conflict, threatening international peace and security.

How is VAWG causally related to state security and insecurity?

Violence is perpetuated by unequal gender relations within and across groups and by the masculine and feminine socialization of individuals and institutions. Together, these dynamics make violence seem not only acceptable but also normative and systemic. It is therefore not surprising that societies with more gender-equal structures are overall less violent, both in terms of state-sanctioned VAWG in the home, at work, or in public and of state engagement in conflict in the name of security or defense. Indeed, a number of scholars of international relations have found that societies with greater gender equality are more peaceful and less likely to go to war or to engage in civil conflict.

We can also view VAWG as a harmful symptom of a patriarchal global governance structure that perpetuates insecurity. In their book *Sex and World Peace*, Valerie Hudson and coauthors argue that the system of male dominance, often called the patriarchy, is not an inevitable social structure. With regard to states and international relations, it produces a highly dysfunctional combination of instability, insecurity, and belligerence, as hypermasculine leaders perceive threats and competition from other states and groups both internally and externally and respond in ways that heighten competition and conflict. Thus, the more a nation-state can establish gender equality in its government and policies—including its foreign policy—the greater the prospects for stability, security, and peace.

Why is there often a spike in VAWG after an international peace agreement or political resolution to conflict?

Conflict endings are typically not the same for women as for men. Often the assumption that the end of conflict results in an end to violence does not take into account VAWG. In fact, violence may increase during a peace negotiation as actors react to the possible end of the conflict and loss of territory, weapons, and war income, or as parties fight toward a mutually hurtful stalemate and seek to inflict maximum damage on the enemy. In both scenarios, this violence is gendered.

There are three main reasons that VAWG tends to increase after the formal cessation of hostilities. First, soldiers returning home from armed conflict can continue to use violence against intimate partners, family members, and others in the community as a means to wield power and assert or reclaim their status. Second, conflict may end, but the presence of politically active women may not, representing a threat to the patriarchal order of many militant groups and new states after conflict. Third, VAWG can be an effective tool to control whole communities in the context of a new regime or leadership, increasing the incidence of violence by threatening them into submission.

In Afghanistan, for instance, substantial increases in femicide, honor killings, and family and intimate partner violence were recorded during the transition of power from the ISAF forces in 2014. According to an Afghanistan Human Rights Commission report (2018), the persistence of violent conflict between Taliban and government forces during the final drawdown of US troops resulted in over 4,000 reported incidents of VAWG, including 277 killings (representing an 8 percent increase in murder of women from the previous year), 12 extrajudicial killing cases, and 1,420 cases of acute physical violence.[3] Similarly, in Colombia, violence against women has substantially increased since the signing of the Final Agreement between the Colombian government and the FARC in 2016.[4] Furthermore, in Syria as the war comes to an end, women's silent endurance of various types of gender-based violence has come to be seen as a form of national resistance and a means to avoid family shame.[5] Unfortunately the cultivation of this silence inevitably means that women and girls continue to be targets of violence as a tactic of political oppression in the post-conflict context. The failure to address impunity as well as inequality in access to social and economic resources during transition accentuates women's insecurity relative to men and, consequently, their vulnerability to violence, especially when displaced or in woman-headed households.

Post-conflict transitions may also perpetuate a culture of impunity for VAWG in legal codes and agreements, exacerbating wider forms of criminal and gendered violence and potentially inciting overtly political violence. Research by the Monash Gender, Peace and Security Centre found that of all the types of gender equality or women's rights provisions in peace agreements, provisions on VAWG were one of the least likely to be implemented. Furthermore, the limited participation of women in peace and security processes, including decision-making, exacerbates their risk of VAWG and aggravates insecurity. For instance, in Aceh, a post-conflict region in Indonesia, the peace agreement that represented the transition from the civil conflict contained no gender equality or women's rights provisions. Moreover, the strict interpretation and practice of Islamic law in the aftermath of conflict has facilitated state-sanctioned violence against women, including public shaming and caning.[6] In Myanmar, another transitional, conflict-affected state, there is still no anti-VAWG law providing clear legal norms and redress for women and girls, despite discussion of its implementation since 2014. In both cases, and in post-conflict countries in general, a spike in VAWG often follows the end of conflict. Crime may be reduced, weapons may be put down, but frictions often persist over land, resources, jobs, and economic development and may have a brutalizing effect on VAWG.

Given this, international actors need to support and incentivize the elimination of impunity for conflict-related VAWG. As the preceding discussion shows, even ostensibly peaceful transitions can maintain the gendered hierarchies present before and during conflict, thereby preventing women from speaking openly about their experiences of violence and from escaping ongoing violence. If gendered violence is then excluded from transitional justice mechanisms and neglected after the guns are silenced, VAWG will continue to harm society.

What is the relationship between VAWG and violent extremism and terrorism?

Violent extremism and terrorism are typically not connected to VAWG by either scholars or commentators. In reality, however, women and girls are often directly targeted by terrorist groups and subjected to gender-based violence. Specifically, the conservative politics of violent extremist groups frequently target women's mobility, dress, marital status, social status, and education, justifying forms of VAWG such as FGM/C or forced marriage as a way of controlling and manipulating women and their communities into submission. Terrorist groups also frequently target women's rights and women's human rights defenders who have established movements to resist extremist activity and reassert their rights. In Libya and Afghanistan, for instance, women leaders have long been targets of extortion, blackmail, and smear campaigns by Islamic extremist groups.

Furthermore, misogynistic attitudes, defined as both fear and hatred of women and/or the feminine, are integral to the ideology, identity, and economy of current violent extremist groups. UN Secretary-General Antonio Guterres has stated that there is a troubling commonality in terrorist attacks, extremist ideologies, and brutal crimes: the violent misogyny of the perpetrators.[7] Many perpetrators of so-called lone wolf terror attacks frequently have a background of domestic violence, as documented in Joan Smith's book *Home Grown*. Indeed, recent research by the Monash Gender, Peace and Security Centre (see Johnson and True 2019) shows that misogyny and support for violence against women are two crucial yet overlooked factors in propelling people to support violent extremist causes. In survey research in Indonesia, Bangladesh, and the Philippines,[8] individuals who supported violence against women were three times more likely to support violent extremism, and this support of violence against women was found to be the strongest of all factors, including education, religiosity, and employment/income, leading to support for violent extremism. While misogyny and violent extremism are connected at the level of individual attitudes, misogyny is also increasingly a part of the gender ideology of violent extremist groups. Specifically, the subordination of women and justifications for VAWG are reflected in extremist groups' publicity campaigns and covert recruitment strategies, which are designed to attract both men and women to their cause. In Indonesia, some extremists have co-opted the language of women's rights in online postings to appeal to women while also promoting gender-discriminatory practices, with the intent of establishing a more devout Islamic state. In Mindanao, the Philippines, IS-affiliated groups have sought to attract women by showing videos of women bearing firearms and shouting *Allahu Akbar* to convey the message that women can be powerful like a man, associating women's empowerment with women's agency to use violence.

While both men and women perpetrate VAWG within the context of violent extremism, gender-based VAWG likely affects women's involvement in violent extremist group in ways that are not yet fully understood. Indeed, women may support violence perpetrated against themselves or other women, including for their own protection, and they may carry out VAWG themselves within violent extremist and terrorist groups (as discussed in chapter 6). In a world that is becoming increasingly globalized and competitive, women's frustrations with unequal and discriminatory gendered social orders that provide little rights or voice for women, such as those experienced by migrant women workers from Indonesia in Hong Kong and the Middle East, may lead them to join violent extremist groups. Such groups that perpetrate violence may provide these women with a sense of belonging and voice, enabling them to take on active roles in fundraising and financing for the group; in logistics such as organizing travel to conflict zones; and in recruiting new members online and social media recruitment as well as, and to a lesser extent, in combat roles.

How does the international security architecture respond to VAWG? What is the Women, Peace and Security agenda?

Armed conflict is experienced differently by women and men because conflict takes place within societies that are fundamentally structured by gender. This insight is the foundation of UN Security Council Resolution (UNSCR) 1325 (2000) on women, peace, and security, and the subsequent eight resolutions that make up the Women, Peace and Security (WPS) agenda. This thematic agenda represents the primary way in which the international security architecture has responded to VAWG, particularly in situations of conflict, post-conflict, violent extremism, and terrorism. The WPS agenda is institutionalized in other UN agencies, intergovernmental institutions (such as NATO, the Organization for Security and Co-operation in Europe, and the African Union), and national action plans adopted by over 80 UN member states.

As the most significant international normative framework to counter VAWG, UNSCR 1325 operates on four pillars: addressing the gender-specific impacts of conflict on women and girls, including protection against sexual and gender-based VAWG; promoting women's participation in peace and security; supporting women's roles as peacebuilders in the prevention of conflict; and ensuring women's rights and participation as part of relief and recovery from conflict and other forms of insecurity. In this sense, as well as responding to conflict-related VAWG, a crucial element of the international security architecture is the recognition and support for women's agency in sustaining peace and preventing violence. There is significant evidence tying women's participation to successful outcomes in peacebuilding, which has implications for transforming highly masculine and male-dominated peace and security decision-making processes. Specifically, women's agency can be effective in brokering and sustaining peace and in bringing a gender equality perspective both to elite roles as peace negotiators and mediators and to collective action outside of formal peace processes. Furthermore, peace agreements are more likely to be signed, implemented, and sustained when women have some form of influence on the process. When women are included in the peace process as part of negotiating parties, the deal is more durable and includes a greater number of provisions related to political change, including reform of national constitutions, political party structures, decentralization and federation processes, civil service arrangements, and judicial systems. One explanation for this is that the collaboration between women delegates and women civil society groups broadens the civilian support base for peace and results in networks that can persistently advocate for the adoption of policies that empower women and reduce VAWG. For example, women in Northern Ireland, Liberia, and the former Yugoslavia have demonstrated a particular capacity to negotiate and overcome ethnic and religious divisions in post-conflict peace processes.

Outside of the formal international security architecture, new informal networks of women leaders have emerged over the past two decades to provide mutual support and mitigate the pressure on women leaders to adopt traditionally masculine repertoires and policy agendas, including the use of force. At the international level, Madeleine Albright began this trend when she created a caucus of female UN ambassadors and a network of female foreign ministers. Most recently, a group of women leaders have formed to defend multilateral institutions from the rise of populism and nationalism. Within many countries including across Africa, informal women's caucuses can be found providing support to women members through capacity-building on policy issues and policymaking, as well as mentoring and networking. Women have also established networks to engage men to become champions of change and gender equality, thus challenging the notion that men will react negatively to women's rights and anti-VAWG advocacy.

Increasingly, we are seeing young women drawing on their experiences of VAWG to emerge as leaders in popular protests against corrupt regimes, material insecurity, sectarianism, hatred, and various types of violence and brutality in their communities. Think of events in Lebanon, Iraq, Iran, Algeria, Libya, and notably, Alaa Saleh, who became the symbol of the Sudanese revolution that overthrew President Omar al-Bashir in 2019. In this revolution from below, ordinary women, from academics and housewives to lawyers and street vendors, played a central role protesting en masse against the regime based on their experiences of genital mutilation and early marriage, demonstrating how experiences of VAWG can be weaponized by survivors to oppose further violence.

Overall, the international WPS architecture is crucial for addressing the attraction of violent extremism, the systemic gender discrimination that provides a fertile ground for radicalization to violence, the use of VAWG as a tactic of violent extremist groups, and the limited spaces for women's participation in countering and preventing violent extremism.

16

VAWG AND HEALTH AND REPRODUCTIVE RIGHTS

What are the health impacts of VAWG?

Violence against women and girls has health consequences that can be immediate and acute, long-lasting and chronic, and even fatal (e.g., from prolonged illness or death due to femicide or suicide). Generally, the more severe the violence, the greater its impacts on women's and girls' physical and mental health. Furthermore, the nonfatal consequences of violence can be far-reaching due to the length of time women endure violence before seeking help. These consequences can also persist long after violence has occurred.

Nonfatal consequences of VAWG include acute or immediate physical injuries, such as bruises, abrasions, lacerations, burns, and broken bones or teeth. They can include sexually transmitted infections such as chlamydia, genital herpes, or HIV, as well as unintended or unwanted pregnancy. Serious physical injuries that result from VAWG can lead to gastrointestinal problems, gynecological disorders, and longer term disabilities, as well as poor health status, reflected in chronic pain and premature death. Likewise, chronic mental health consequences that can result from VAWG include depression, sleeping and eating disorders, stress and anxiety disorders (such as PTSD), low self-esteem, self-harm, and suicidal ideation. Finally, behavioral consequences, including alcohol or substance abuse and disorders, panic attacks, and concentration problems, can further compound the direct health impacts of VAWG.

Australia's National Organisation for Women's Safety (ANROWS) found that intimate partner violence is the greatest health risk factor for Australian women aged 18–44, contributing more to the burden of disease (that is, the impact of illness, disability, and premature death) than any other risk factor, including smoking, alcohol, and obesity.[1] Furthermore, a systematic review of 43 studies found strong evidence that women who experienced intimate partner violence had an increased risk of depression, pregnancy termination, and femicide. There was also evidence of a relationship between intimate partner violence and alcohol and drug abuse, as well as preterm birth and low birth weight in babies.

These findings are consistent with the global findings of WHO (2013) that women who have been physically or sexually abused by their intimate partners are more likely to have a low birth weight baby, more than twice as likely to have an abortion, almost twice as likely to experience depression, and in some regions, one and half times more likely to acquire HIV. The health outcomes for the estimated 7 percent of women globally who have been sexually assaulted by a nonpartner are even worse: such women are 2.3 times more likely to have alcohol use disorders and 2.6 times more likely to experience depression or anxiety. Overall, as shown by the myriad harms and health problems mentioned, VAWG has a significant impact on its victims.

What are the intergenerational health impacts of VAWG on children and other family members of victims, including men and boys?

Women in violent relationships frequently have children in their care, and a significant proportion report their children having witnessed the acts of intimate partner violence. Based on a US national sample survey of 4,503 children aged 17 and under, McTavish and colleagues found that 17 percent of children reported having witnessed a parent assault another caregiver in their lifetimes, and 6 percent had witnessed a parent assault another caregiver in the past year.[2] Children who are exposed to violence in the home may suffer a range of severe and lasting effects. According to UNICEF, children who grow up in a home with violence are more likely to be victims of child abuse, and those who are not direct victims may share some of the same behavioral and psychological issues as children who have experienced physical abuse.[3] For instance, children who are exposed to violence in the home may have difficulty learning, exhibit violent or risky behavior, possess limited social skills, or suffer from anxiety and depression. They are also at increased risk of psychological, social, emotional, and behavioral problems, including mood, anxiety and stress disorders, substance abuse, and education-related problems.

As well as witnessing violence perpetrated against women, children can also be the direct target of it. This situation may arise when the child intervenes in the violence that is occurring or attempts to protect the mother or female caregiver from it, or the child may be specifically targeted by the perpetrator. According to Bourget, Grace, and Whitehurst (2007), up to 20 percent of filicide cases (especially paternal filicide) involve a history of domestic VAWG. Childhood experiences of domestic and family violence can lead to greater likelihood of adult experiences of violence and negative mental and physical health outcomes, possibly as a result of trauma and cumulative harm through long-term exposure to violence. Specifically, experiencing VAWG may impact children's ability to form attachments and develop healthy relationships due to the normalization of violence in the relationships modeled to them. Re-victimization through violence and abuse may also be a common outcome for sufferers of trauma, particularly for children who have suffered multiple forms of abuse.

If left untreated, trauma symptoms can result in psychosocial and physical responses that have long-lasting effects on children's development, behavior, and well-being. In many ways, these symptoms reflect those suffered by the victim of the initial violence (if not the children themselves), and include depression, low self-esteem, anxiety, poor coping mechanisms, suicidal thoughts, eating disorders, self-harm, substance use and abuse, and chronic pain. According to Price-Robertson and colleagues (2013), sustained and chronic exposure to domestic VAWG can result in trauma that distorts survivors' sense of identity and concept of others, leading to mistrust, social isolation, and difficulty relating to others.

Various studies have found that childhood experiences of domestic VAWG also increase the likelihood of adult homelessness. For instance, data from the Journeys Home study (see Scutella and colleagues 2014) shows that people who are homeless or in insecure housing have also experienced high rates of childhood neglect and physical and sexual abuse, and that childhood abuse is associated with longer durations of homelessness. Indeed, having lived in a violent home environment increases not only the risk of homelessness but also the risk of experiencing physical and sexual victimization on the streets perpetrated by partners and other known or unknown perpetrators.

Some studies have shown an association between exposure to domestic VAWG for boys and the risk of perpetrating partner aggression later in life. However, it is unlikely that exposure to this domestic violence alone explains perpetration of VAWG. Not all children who witness or experience abuse or family violence go on to become perpetrators; likewise, a significant proportion of men who are violent toward women have not experienced or witnessed such violence as children. The reasons men use VAWG are complex. Men's and boys' risk of perpetrating VAWG is mediated by a range of social and structural factors, including violence-supportive attitudes; structural inequalities; gendered power imbalances;

and harmful gender norms, such as forms of masculinity as- sociated with power, control, domination, aggression, and sexual entitlement. In this sense, the intergenerational effects of VAWG cannot be understood without being placed in their wider social, economic, and political contexts.

What are the reproductive health impacts of VAWG?

Violence against women and girls has significant effects on women's sexual and reproductive health. A systematic review by the Guttmacher Institute links intimate partner violence, sexual VAWG, and a lack of reproductive control to negative sexual and reproductive health outcomes for women, espe- cially those who are young and poor. Rape as a particular form of VAWG is an important contributor to women's reproductive vulnerability, including to sexually transmitted infections like HIV. This can arise through non-consensual sexual intercourse, as well as women's inability to control the timing of inter- course or to negotiate the use of condoms. Behavioral evidence suggests that men who use violence against female partners are more likely than nonviolent men to engage in HIV-risk be- haviors (e.g., having unprotected sex with multiple partners, lacking awareness of or diligence regarding sexual health), which can also increase women's risk of contracting HIV.

Relationships that involve VAWG are often marked by fear and controlling behaviors by partners, and women in these relationships report poorer sexual and reproductive health outcomes. Importantly, these heightened rates of adverse re- productive events are not just the direct result of sexual vio- lence and coercion, but also arise from more indirect pathways affecting contraceptive use, such as the sabotage and preven- tion of birth control measures. As a result, the rate of unin- tended pregnancy is higher in women who are experiencing violent relationships; WHO (2013) reports that of approxi- mately 80 million unintended pregnancies each year, at least half are terminated through induced abortion, and of those terminations, nearly half take place in unsafe conditions. While there are risks associated with unintended pregnancy carried to term, illegal and unsafe abortion practices are particularly dangerous to women's health.

In addition, VAWG has a negative impact on the health of pregnant women and new mothers and their infants. Specifically, low birth weight in newborns has been shown to, among other things, be connected to heightened stress. Living in an abusive and dangerous environment marked by chronic stress can therefore be an important risk factor for maternal and infant health. Furthermore, intimate partner violence among women prior to or during pregnancy has been linked to several pregnancy complications. For instance, women experiencing intimate partner violence are at greater risk for rapid or repeat pregnancies, which excludes them from the health benefits of planning and spacing pregnancies. In addition, experiences of intimate partner violence lower the rate at which women seek out prenatal care both before becoming or while pregnant, and Mogos and coauthors (2016) found that having experienced intimate partner violence before delivery was associated with four times the probability of stillbirth.

Negative reproductive health outcomes for women may also arise from the psychological control that defines many relationships involving VAWG. Evidence suggests that violent partners who exhibit controlling behaviors, such as limiting women's social and family interactions and insisting on knowing a woman's location at all times, can impede women's ability to control their sexual and reproductive decision-making and access to healthcare, which can result in several of the aforementioned adverse health effects.

Finally, it has been suggested that sexual VAWG is a reproductive health issue because it functions as an assault on a woman's sexual and reproductive health *in and of itself*, regardless of the reproductive impacts. A broad definition of sexual and reproductive health and rights is upheld in international norms such as those established by CEDAW and includes the right to bodily integrity and to enjoyable and satisfying sexual relations free of discrimination, coercion, and violence. In this sense, the reproductive health of a woman who experiences intimate partner violence is severely compromised regardless of whether it results in an adverse reproductive health outcome, such as a sexually transmitted infection, unwanted pregnancy, or other complications.

Part 4

RESPONSES

17

LEGAL FRAMEWORKS

NATIONAL AND INTERNATIONAL

*What national laws cover VAWG? In how many countries is
VAWG still not a crime?*

National laws covering VAWG vary drastically throughout
the world. In some countries, they are extremely comprehensive; in others, there remain large gaps that leave more women
and girls vulnerable to violence. The World Bank's report
on women's economic opportunity and rights first piloted a
Protecting Women from Violence legal indicator in 2014. Based
on a survey of governments, experts, and civil society moni-
tors, the World Bank analyzed the extent and scope of laws in
100 countries on domestic violence (physical, sexual, psychological, and economic) and sexual harassment in schools and
public places. In 2014 it found that 76 out of 100 countries had
domestic violence legislation, while 32 countries had legislation on sexual harassment in schools and 8 countries had laws
prohibiting sexual harassment in public spaces.[1] By 2017 the
same survey found a nearly 50 percent increase in the anti-
VAWG laws adopted, with 107 countries legislating on domestic violence and 57 with legislation on sexual harassment
in schools. The number of countries with sexual harassment in
public spaces laws also increased to 25. However, 69 countries
still did not have any laws against economic violence, and just
35 countries covered all forms of violence as well as violence
perpetrated by unmarried intimate partners.[2]

It is important to note that a number of countries were excluded from the Protecting Women from Violence study, mostly due to the lack of data given their small size or incomplete data gathering. However, several countries had no laws at all to prevent domestic violence, sexual violence, or harassment: Republic of Congo, Djibouti, Equatorial Guinea, Eswatini (Swaziland), Gabon, Haiti, Liberia, Mali, Mauritania, Federated States of Micronesia, and Russia. While conjecture is difficult without data, we would expect that countries with no laws or policies to prevent VAWG have lower awareness and possibly higher rates of VAWG (though not necessarily higher rates of reported violence) due to the normalized nature of the problem and the lack of institutions to receive reports of violence.

The United States is a positive case of legal and other means of redress having become readily available to victims/survivors. In 1994 Congress passed the Violence Against Women Act (VAWA), which was reauthorized in 2005. This act recognizes that domestic violence is a national crime and creates federal laws to assist state and local criminal justice systems in dealing with domestic violence. In 1994 and 1996 Congress also passed changes to the Gun Control Act, making it a federal crime in certain situations for domestic violence abusers to have guns in their possession. Furthermore, an appropriations bill in 2011 included significant funding and guidance to state and local authorities for domestic violence services, including those related to temporary housing, employment programs, and other social services. While most domestic violence cases continue to be handled by state and local authorities, in some cases federal laws (and the remedies gained from them) may be the most appropriate course of action.

Conversely, let us assess a country in which there is no legal redress: Russia. Russia does not have a national domestic violence law, and domestic violence is not listed as a separate offense in either the criminal or administrative codes. In fact, in 2017 Russia decriminalized domestic violence, overturning its previous law. Battery offenses by a partner are now treated in the same way as battery offenses committed by nonfamily members—that is, as an administrative offense with very mild penalties. The 2017 amendments seemed to promote domestic violence by reducing penalties for perpetrators, making it harder for women to bring charges against perpetrators and weakening their protections from further violence. Indeed, the lack of a separate domestic violence offense reinforces the impression held by many that Russian authorities do not view domestic violence as a significant crime. Importantly, this has public, rather than simply private, ramifications because it sends the message to all Russian men that what goes on in their homes is largely their own business, and the state will be unlikely to step in to protect women or other family members from violence. Russian authorities have even alleged at the European Court of Human Rights that men in Russia suffered from discrimination because men are not expected to seek protection, particularly if the perpetrator is female, as well as that the problem of domestic violence has been exaggerated.[3]

The World Bank indicates that there are also 27 countries that have sexual harassment legislation but no domestic violence or explicit prohibition against marital rape legislation. One such country is Afghanistan, which is reflected in the fact that 87 percent of women and girls in Afghanistan experience abuse in their lifetimes, according to Global Rights, a research institute in Washington, DC.[4] This is particularly the case for physical violence. In 2018, UN researchers studying 932 married women in Afghanistan found that 23 percent had experienced physical violence from their husbands in the previous 12 months.[5] Although the Law on the Elimination of Violence against Women (EVAW) was passed in 2009, few cases have managed to reach a court in Afghanistan due to Islamic family law structures being used as the primary fora for resolving domestic disputes. The legal process is further hampered by procedural issues, such as criminal code limitations that prohibit judicial authorities from questioning the relatives of a criminal defendant. This legal framework effectively silences victims of domestic violence, as well as their family members who may have witnessed the abuse, thereby undermining the purpose and implementation of EVAW.

Other countries reveal surprising gaps in laws on domestic violence and marital rape. For instance, in Singapore, rape in marriage has been explicitly excluded from rape laws except in very narrow circumstances, such as following separation or when a court has issued a protection order against the husband. However, husbands who force their wives to have intercourse may be prosecuted under assault laws. Importantly, a reform bill is currently under consideration in the Singaporean Parliament to abolish the marital rape exclusion, and it is expected to come into effect in 2020. Similarly, in India, marital rape is outside of the definition of rape, and forced sex in marriage is only a crime when the wife is under the age of 16. Far from reforming the law, both male and female legislators in the Indian parliament have argued that criminalizing marital rape has the potential to destroy the institution of marriage and the Indian family structure—arguments not unlike those raised in Russia.

As the preceding discussion shows, different countries have different legislative provisions to address various forms of VAWG. Ultimately, the inconsistency across the world in legislating to prevent VAWG is problematic, as it has meant that women face confusing, sometimes plural, legal schemes and lack clear legal protections and remedies when seeking out justice against perpetrators.

What redress do victims of VAWG have under national law?

Even in countries with strong legislation, implementation remains a serious problem, as domestic violence laws are often not sufficiently budgeted for and face resistance from the male-dominated judiciary and police. If justice system personnel (including judges, police, and forensic doctors) have gender-inequitable or victim-blaming attitudes, this can deter women from seeking help through formal mechanisms, and if they do seek help, it can have a direct impact on the outcomes for women.

For example, in the United States, a federal domestic violence victim under VAWA has a number of rights, including the right to speak to the judge at a bail hearing to inform her or him of any danger posed by the release of the defendant. Any victim of a violent crime also has the right to address the court in person at the time of sentencing. If a charge is upheld, the court must order restitution (i.e., compensation) to pay the victim the full amount of loss. Notably, the calculation of loss from domestic violence is wide-ranging; it includes costs associated with medical or psychological care, physical therapy, transport, temporary housing, child care, loss of income, legal fees, costs incurred in obtaining other protection mechanisms (e.g., a civil protection order), and any other losses suffered by the victim as a result of the offense. Furthermore, as victims of domestic violence living in public housing sometimes face unfair eviction and denial of housing benefits, the 2005 VAWA reauthorization passed new provisions to protect victims from housing discrimination and allow them to access the criminal justice system while maintaining their housing. Specifically, these protections permit housing agencies to prioritize victims for housing when their safety dictates, while also prohibiting housing agencies from denying housing to a victim or evicting that person on the basis of domestic violence.

In contrast, access to justice for VAWG remains limited in Asia and the Pacific, reflecting a lack of the requisite policies and mechanisms for meaningful enforcement. Services that should be provided to victims under the law are often not available, and the existence of both formal and traditional justice systems creates an added complexity for victims in accessing justice. Specifically, many Asia-Pacific countries still have cultural, customary, or religious laws and dispute frameworks that are conducive to or legitimate violence against women. There is little coordination between formal and informal systems of justice, and the justice afforded in the formal versus informal institutions can be very different in the same country, which is a key issue for victims' access to redress in law. Location, socioeconomic status, ethnicity, and religious identity may further determine which system of justice women can access. While women tend to access informal justice institutions more than formal ones, this should not be confused with their preference; rather, when formal institutions are available (in terms of location) and accessible (in terms of cost), women seek these services above informal mechanisms for justice.

What redress do victims of VAWG have under international law?

International and regional human rights and policy instruments set out states' obligations to combat all forms of discrimination against women, including VAWG, and to protect their human rights, including every woman's right to live free from violence. These include the obligation to protect women and girls from gender-based violence, particularly in the context of domestic violence or intimate partner violence, by ensuring their safety and human rights through access to shelters and protection orders. Furthermore, women and girls who have been victims of violence may seek recourse under international law to hold the state responsible for violence perpetrated against them—specifically, its failure to prevent, investigate, prosecute, and punish such acts.

Under articles 1 and 2 of CEDAW, states have an obligation to prevent, investigate, prosecute, and punish acts of discrimination against women, which includes gender-based VAWG, and to provide remedies to victims. Closely linked to this prevention obligation is the requirement that states provide adequate protection to victims and potential victims of violence. Furthermore, states and their national bodies and agencies are required to refrain from engaging in any act or practice that discriminates against women and must ensure that public authorities and institutions conform with this obligation.

Critically, states also have a "due diligence" obligation in international law related to discrimination and violence against women perpetrated by nonstate actors, including private persons. This due diligence obligation includes adequate implementation of anti-VAWG laws and robust criminal justice responses involving the cooperation of all state actors. Under General Recommendation No. 19, CEDAW further explains that states may also be responsible for private acts or acts of violence occurring in private spaces (as they are for acts occurring publicly) if they fail to act with due diligence to prevent rights violations or to investigate and penalize acts of violence.

In a similar fashion, the Council of Europe's Istanbul Convention, ratified by 34 countries across Europe, explicitly refers to violence against women as a human rights violation and protects the right of everyone, particularly women, to live free from violence in both public and private spheres. This recognition creates a human rights obligation among states to protect women victims or potential victims of violence by adopting laws and practical measures to prevent and combat such violence. It also requires the provision of a comprehensive set of social services, such as shelters and refuges, as well as judicial responses, including protection orders.

As discussed in chapter 5, redress is also available at the international level for sexual violence and gender-based crimes committed during armed conflict under the Rome Statute of the International Criminal Court (ICC). Specifically, the ICC has established mechanisms to ensure that its Victims and Witnesses Unit provides protection, support, and other appropriate assistance to safeguard those giving testimony, including measures to protect personal safety, physical and psychological well-being, dignity, and privacy. Furthermore, the ICC's Trust Fund for Victims is mandated to assist victims and administer court-ordered reparations. It is hoped that doing so will enable victims of VAWG in the context of genocide, crimes of humanity, war crimes, and aggression to return to dignified and meaningful lives within their communities.

When can we see states being held responsible for VAWG?

The Optional Protocol of CEDAW (OP-CEDAW) establishes complaint and inquiry procedures to hold states accountable for VAWG. Through the OP-CEDAW's complaint procedure, individuals or groups of individuals can bring alleged violations of the Convention to the CEDAW Committee. Importantly, this requires victims to have exhausted domestic remedies (e.g., by first seeking legal recourse in national courts). The case of *Angela González Carreño v. Spain* (2014) illustrates the circumstances in which a state is held responsible for VAWG perpetrated within its borders. This case was brought as an individual complaint case under OP-CEDAW due to the failure of the Spanish courts to take effective action to prevent domestic violence. In this case, Angela's ex-husband used the legal custody process to harass Angela and her daughter Andrea, and eventually killed the child during an unsupervised custody visit. The CEDAW Committee concluded that the violence committed against Angela and the murder of Andrea were foreseeable given Angela's repeated complaints to police, and that failures in Spain's justice structures and practices (such as by allowing unsupervised custody visits) led to both Angela and Andrea being denied appropriate protection. Consequently, reparations were awarded to Angela.

As a result of states being held responsible, some survivors are eligible for compensation when states fail to protect against gender-based violence as a form of discrimination against women under international law. One example is the case of *Opuz v. Turkey* (2009), brought before the European Court of Human Rights. In this case, Ms. Opuz and her mother suffered years of extreme violence from Ms. Opuz's husband, including beatings, stabbings, and attempted murder using a car. Despite their complaints to the police and authorities, little was done to protect the women: Turkish authorities only temporarily detained the husband after some incidents, viewing the matter as a private family issue to be resolved at home. Ms. Opuz's mother was eventually killed by her son-in-law, after the women had again sought help from police only one month earlier. At trial, the court unanimously found that the responses of the authorities to these complaints of domestic violence were "manifestly inadequate" in that they failed to appropriately punish the husband and protect both Ms. Opuz and her mother from cruel, inhuman, and degrading treatment. The court found that the state's failure to address domestic violence constituted a form of gender-based discrimination. To compensate, it awarded Ms. Opuz nonpecuniary damages for the anguish and distress suffered and additional damages for the authorities' failure to engage sufficient measures to prevent the domestic violence perpetrated by her husband.

Who is responsible for VAWG if a state is recalcitrant?

Unfortunately there are numerous instances in which states fail in their duty to effectively and appropriately investigate and punish acts of VAWG, particularly with regard to violence committed in the private sphere. The pervasiveness of patriarchal attitudes in the law enforcement and justice systems, coupled with a lack of resources and insufficient knowledge of existing applicable legislation, often leads to inadequate responses to VAWG and deepens the persistent social acceptance of such acts.

As mentioned previously, some states still have not criminalized all manifestations of VAWG, including sexual violence within marriage and other forms of domestic violence, leaving women vulnerable to abuse and without legal recourse. In some cases, unless violence results in serious physical injuries

(or even if it does), the police, prosecutors, and judges can minimize offences in the belief that domestic violence is a private
matter. Victims may therefore be discouraged by authorities
from pursuing legal action against perpetrators, instead being
offered mediation and reconciliation or otherwise being encouraged to return to situations of abuse. In some jurisdictions,
cases of domestic violence are treated as administrative rather
than criminal offences or are classified as misdemeanors, resulting in mild or administrative sentences for perpetrators.
For instance, Human Rights Watch has criticized Algerian law
for relying excessively on assessments of physical incapacitation to determine sentencing, without offering medical guidelines on how to determine incapacitation in domestic violence
cases. As these examples show, unless states establish a comprehensive and victim-oriented justice mechanism to prosecute, prevent, and protect against VAWG, vulnerable women
and girls will continue to face abuse without reprieve.

18

POLICY FRAMEWORKS AND SOLUTIONS

How can we protect victims of VAWG?

The protection of victims is a central pillar of policy responses to VAWG and an obligation of all states in international law. Protection requires the delivery of an effective criminal justice system, as well as the provision of services to help women deal with and/or leave violent situations, including telephone hotlines, counseling centers, legal assistance, shelters, protection orders, and financial aid.

Many victims of repetitive violence, such as intimate partner violence or stalking, have an increased need for protection against their offenders. Protection orders (otherwise known as domestic violence orders or restraining orders) are a common legal response to VAWG and aim to prevent the recurrence of violence by restricting perpetrator contact or activity with victims. While protection orders are typically issued under civil proceedings, police are responsible for their enforcement and are expected to investigate any breach and charge offenders as criminals. For example, the European Union has recently introduced an EU-wide protection order to ensure safety and support for victims of domestic violence and prevent harassment across borders. The regulation means that women who are citizens of one country in the EU and have suffered domestic violence can rely on a restraining order obtained in their home country wherever they are in the EU; in other words, the protection travels across the countries of the EU with the citizen.

Survivors of VAWG require both immediate and ongoing protective support. This may include support in seeking access to healthcare providers, justice systems, and general information about VAWG in order to make informed choices. Crisis centers and support programs can provide a range of essential services in one place—often coined "one-stop-shop" crisis centers—to ensure that women and children are safely removed from violent situations and receive a range of supports. For example, Women Against Violence Against Women (WAVAW) is the largest rape crisis center operating in British Colombia, Canada, offering trauma-informed support to survivors of sexual violence. Its services include a 24-hour crisis and info line, hospital accompaniment, police and court accompaniment, and counseling. It also offers workshops and resources to universities, schools, community organizations, and service providers seeking to expand their knowledge about supporting survivors and increase their awareness of damaging gender norms and the intersectional forms of discrimination that women and girls may face.

More recently, India has introduced a smattering of one-stop-shop crisis centers for women and girls who are victims of gender-based violence. Their establishment followed the recommendations of the 2013 Justice Verma Commission, which arose as a result of the fatal gang rape of a twenty-three-year-old female tertiary student on a Delhi bus in December 2012. Initially these centers were intended to serve only victims of sexual violence; however, the majority of clients have turned out to be victims of domestic violence, demonstrating the need for government anti-VAWG measures to understand what risks women face and what forms of protection are most appropriate to their situations.

Finally, programs for known perpetrators of VAWG are an important step toward protecting victims. Dedicated perpetrator intervention programs include men's behavior change programs and other community-based responses, as well as interventions in the context of criminal justice, child protection, and family law systems. For example, the Caledonian System in Scotland involves a behavioral change program for men convicted of domestic abuse offenses, as well as support, safety planning, and advocacy services for their partners and children.[1] The Men's Program lasts at least two years and comprises a minimum of 14 one-on-one preparation and motivation sessions, a group work stage of at least 26 weekly three-hour sessions, and further post-group one-on-one work. Participation is a mandatory requirement of a statutory order or license; perpetrators are referred by court order if convicted of domestic violence offences and assessed as suitable candidates in terms of risk and willingness to change. In 2016 the Caledonian Men's Program received positive evaluations and was reaccredited by the Scottish Advisory Panel on Offender Rehabilitation for five years from December 2017.

How effective is prosecution as a strategy for deterring and therefore reducing VAWG?

Impunity for VAWG is a systemic problem; therefore, laws and policies that address this impunity through the prosecution of perpetrators are crucial for preventing or deterring future crimes. It is difficult to judge whether increased prosecution leads to reduction in VAWG crimes because so many crimes go unreported, affecting the accuracy of any measurement of the impact of prosecution. However, with increased prosecution we would expect to see increased reporting of VAWG, in the sense that victims will be more willing to report crimes given the prospect of redress vis-à-vis their perpetrators. Moreover, with appropriate institutional capacity to protect victims and prosecute perpetrators, national laws to eliminate VAWG and government action plans to implement them directly target the culture of impunity surrounding VAWG, thereby helping to reduce and prevent violence.

The justice sector has a powerful role to play in a coordinated response to ending VAWG. However, in a number of countries the successful prosecution of perpetrators of VAWG has been undermined by factors that include gaps in legislative frameworks that fail to cover all types of VAWG (see chapter 17), male-dominated judiciaries and police forces, gender inequitable and/or victim-blaming attitudes in the justice system, inefficient or insufficient resources, and prioritization of informal justice mechanisms over formal justice mechanisms (e.g., mediation and reconciliation or, most egregiously, the marriage of victims to perpetrators). These undermining factors are being addressed in many ways. For instance, following the adoption of a law to eliminate VAWG in India, a civil society initiative supported by transnational advocacy networks and the UN set up a system to monitor the implementation of the law in collaboration with state agencies. The Lawyers Collective, along with other organizations and stakeholders, evaluated the effectiveness of the infrastructure envisaged by the Protection of Women from Domestic Violence Act and the performance of the implementing agencies. They also examined the responsiveness of the judiciary to the issue of VAWG. This initiative has substantially increased the state's accountability to civil society in deterring and reducing VAWG.

Many countries also have extremely low VAWG conviction rates, which means that prosecution cannot be a foolproof strategy for reducing violence. In India, only 3,860 of the 5,337 rape cases of women and girls reported over a 10-year period resulted in prosecutions.[2] According to the Indian National Crime Records Bureau, perpetrators were either acquitted or discharged by the courts due to lack of proper evidence.[3] In Indonesia, the CEDAW Committee has voiced concern over the limited number of cases of sexual violence and trafficking brought to court, and as yet there is no monitoring mechanism for their domestic violence law. Furthermore, a UN study of nine countries in Asia found that the majority of men in the region face no legal consequences for committing physical or sexual VAWG, which reflects the pervasive gender inequalities in the law and justice system that continue to hamper efforts to end VAWG.[4]

In response to low conviction rates, some countries have established specialist courts for gender-based VAWG cases. In 2014 in Nepal, for instance, the Supreme Court mandated the establishment of fast-track courts for rape and domestic violence, in addition to the on-camera (rather than in-person) hearings provided for in the Domestic Violence Crime and Punishment Act. Women often experience double victimization in court when they are expected to testify before their perpetrators, whose accounts are given equal weight. The on-camera hearings attempt to rectify this impact on victims, which otherwise may deter them from seeking legal justice in the first place. Similar provisions were introduced in 2015 in New South Wales, Australia, which permitted police to take video statements from survivors of domestic violence incidents to be used in court as evidence. As in Nepal, this procedure was designed to spare survivors the stress and traumatization of having to give evidence in person at court, as well as to increase the number of successful prosecutions for VAWG.

Another response to low prosecution rates is to establish specialized policing to increase the reporting and prosecution of VAWG-related crimes. The presence of female staff at all stages of the VAWG response process may be helpful in reducing VAWG, as it has been found that both male and female victims of sexual violence prefer to report to women police. In a study of 39 countries, the UN reported that the presence of women police officers correlated positively with reporting of sexual assault. This finding confirms that recruiting women is an important component of a gender-responsive justice system. It does not, however, excuse justice systems from undertaking comprehensive and gender-sensitive training for all members of the police to ensure that victims are appropriately and mindfully dealt with at all stages of seeking justice.

There is a growing body of evidence to show that women's police stations or units reduce some of the systemic problems entrenched in the current male-dominated models of policing VAWG. These women's units are especially prevalent in Latin America, although they have also been initiated in the Philippines and India, indicating global potential. For example, born from demands that Brazil advance women's citizenship by protecting them from male violence, between 1985 and 2010 São Paulo established around 475 specialist women's police stations. Perova and Reynolds assessed shifts in female homicide rates in 2,074 Brazilian municipalities between 2004 and 2009, finding that where women's specialist police stations existed, the female homicide rate dropped by 17 percent for all women and by 50 percent for women aged 15–24 in metropolitan areas. Other Latin American countries have also now prioritized women's police stations, resulting in the establishment of 128 women's police stations in Buenos Aires, Argentina, by the end of 2018. Kerry Carrington and her colleagues (2019) conducted research into 10 of these women's police stations and found that their performance was effective in enhancing women's willingness to report violence, thereby increasing the likelihood of conviction and enlarging access to a range of other services for victims, such as counseling, health, legal, financial, and social support.

Prosecution will only be an effective strategy to deter and reduce VAWG if it is undertaken in a gender-sensitive way. For instance, gender mainstreaming (which aims to integrate a differentiated assessment of policies on women and men) within the prosecution agency, including the use of standardized protocols for handling VAWG cases and gender sensitivity training for prosecutors, can contribute to the prevention of VAWG. In England and Wales, this institutional culture awareness is visible in an Expectations Statement for the Bar, which provides a clear and concise statement of expectations about equality and diversity for prosecutors when working for the state prosecution service. Furthermore, while increasing the number of women in justice institutions is no guarantee of a corresponding increase in women's access to justice, there is evidence to suggest that increasing the number of female judges, female police, and other frontline justice sector officials can create more conducive environments for women in courts and make a difference to the outcome of sexual violence cases.

In her book *Decriminalizing Domestic Violence*, Leigh Goodmark argues that reliance on criminal prosecution to deter and reduce VAWG is an ineffective approach. Specifically, Goodmark argues that doing so directs the state's resources away from addressing the political economy–related causes of violence rooted in gender inequality and other structural inequalities, thereby absolving the state from its responsibility to confront them. While incarceration reduces the life chances of the former prisoner, Goodmark notes that it also destroys the lives of those connected to the prisoner, including family members. Moreover, criminalization affords limited protection to the women and girls who are its intended beneficiaries, many of whom wish to move on with their lives and avoid situations of violence. There is, finally, little evidence to suggest that criminalization prevents intimate partner violence, one of the major types of VAWG.

In this context, survivor-centered perspectives suggest that criminal prosecution should operate as just one strategy— rather than the main strategy—for reducing and preventing VAWG. Other policy interventions should include promoting human rights and nonviolence education for all citizens, providing economic resources to survivors through cash transfers and other mobilization programs, the creation and upkeep of secure housing, increased minimum wages, skills/training workshops to help survivors gain employment and to rehabilitate abusers, and community-based support measures to increase intervention efficacy and provide opportunities for restorative justice and accountability.

What works in preventing VAWG?

Prevention needs to be at the center of all efforts to eliminate VAWG, not only because it is more cost-effective but because it addresses the root causes of the problem. States have fundamental obligations to protect, respect, and fulfill the human rights of all women and girls, including the right to live free from violence (see chapter 17). The positive duty to ensure these rights is integral to the prevention of VAWG and a far better way of achieving long-term, sustainable reductions in violence than protection or prosecution alone. While prevention strategies need to respond to local contexts, they must all target the underlying social acceptance of VAWG that contributes to its prevalence and focus on achieving the empowerment and equal status of women in all societies.

Proactive interventions to prevent VAWG are as important as services for those who need help after the violence has occurred. Three of these types of interventions are highlighted here: awareness-raising campaigns, youth education, and early identification/intervention and training.

Awareness-raising campaigns are a primary and effective means of prevention. They are designed to challenge attitudes and debunk common myths about VAWG. In the past, campaigns have focused on providing information for women experiencing violence rather than on educating the general public about the reality of VAWG as a social problem. Campaigns at local and national levels need to challenge social attitudes and the secrecy and stigma that surround VAWG in order to bring it into the public domain, where it can be meaningfully addressed. Similarly, changing the attitudes of men, particularly of those most likely to condone or involve themselves in VAWG, is critical. For example, in the United States, initiatives that incorporate components of cultural and social norm change have been developed to reduce dating violence and sexual abuse among teenagers. Men of Strength clubs, Mentors in Violence Prevention, and Men Against Violence programs (targeting both men and women) are all initiatives that acknowledge the strong influence of young adults on their peers' behaviors and unpack the social pressures of masculinity that equate male power and status with violence.

Educating and safeguarding children and young people is another successful means of prevention. This includes supporting the promotion of healthy relationships, gender equality, and nonviolence through working with children and young people in schools (as discussed in chapter 13), as well as programs with adults—for example, through parenting guidance and family support initiatives. In many countries, schools have an existing statutory duty to develop and implement behavioral, antibullying, and gender equality policies, creating a strong framework for schools to counteract VAWG. For example, Canada's Fourth R program is designed on the understanding that relationship knowledge and skills can and should be taught in the same way as reading, writing, and arithmetic (hence the Fourth R, for relationships). It seeks to help older secondary and tertiary students learn skills for healthy relationships and raise their expectations for respectful relationships by better identifying the warning signs of abuse. A five-year randomized control trial of this program indicated reduced use of violence and shifts in norms, demonstrating its potential as a tool for early violence prevention.[5]

Early identification/intervention and training in communities and workplaces is also essential for the prevention of VAWG. For example, the Warehouse Group Ltd., the largest retail group operating in New Zealand, provides a safe place on its trading site that connects people to women's refuges and information about family violence, all of which cannot be traced.[6] Management teams are all trained in spotting signs of violence and how best to assist victims, and the company's intranet contains detailed information about family violence and methods for getting help.

Promoting early intervention across public services is also an important step to minimize the harm to women and children at risk of violence. Women and girls who are victims of violence will likely come into contact with several public services (e.g., hospital services, school counselors), so it is important that professionals in these areas be trained to spot risk factors or early indications of violence, such as incidence of family breakdown, teenage pregnancy, alcohol and drug abuse, smoking, absenteeism, and school drop-out.

Which interventions have made the most difference in reducing VAWG in recent years?

Myriad reforms and interventions have been carried out in order to combat VAWG. Some approaches that have been found to be particularly effective are anti-VAWG interventions that combine transformations in gender relations and household economies, as well as anti-VAWG education programs that mobilize communities around social norms change.

Structural interventions linking economic strengthening to gender transformation are increasingly being recognized as critical to tackling the intersections of women's risk of and vulnerability to violence. Specifically, studies have shown that gender-transformative social change interventions combined with economic empowerment interventions can have a significant impact in reducing VAWG. For example, International Alert and its partners implemented the Zindagii Shoista project in Tajikistan across four villages, involving around 270 people from 80 families.[7] Zindagii Shoista was developed as an innovative family-centered social and economic intervention tailored to the Tajik context, in which 60 percent of women had been found to have experienced violence in the previous 12 months. The program involved 10 weeks of social empowerment sessions focused on family values and attitudes toward gender and relationships, including raising awareness of VAWG. Following this, participants undertook 10 weeks of economic empowerment activities to build an understanding of women's contribution to household economics, strengthen financial management skills, and boost household livelihoods by encouraging families to engage in their own income-generating activities. This integrated approach was effective in reducing domestic violence and intimate partner violence over a period of 15 months: there was a reduction in women's reports of experiencing violence from 64 to 33 percent and in men's reports of perpetrating violence from 48 to 5 percent. Furthermore, depression rates were cut in half (and male suicide rates were cut to zero), while women's earnings quadrupled and levels of food insecurity significantly decreased. Ultimately, the results of the Zindagii Shoista intervention reveal the significant impact of gender-transformative social change interventions combined with economic empowerment interventions in reducing VAWG, with additional benefits arising for participants' emotional well-being, family dynamics, and economic security.

Another policy approach that has proven effective in reducing VAWG is community mobilization around social norms change. Community-based structures can be harnessed to raise public awareness about the drivers and consequences of VAWG and to reduce VAWG through transforming the norms and attitudes that underpin its perpetration. Community-based anti-VAWG intervention has been achieved by mobilizing a group of respected male and female community members to facilitate anti-VAWG activities. For example, a rural response system intervention in Ghana established community-based action teams (COMBATs) made up of community members trained to facilitate activities around gender, VAWG, and the law, as well as to provide counseling for couples experiencing violence. The COMBATs received five days of training on gender sensitivity, VAWG, and the national Domestic Violence Act, as well as on important fields of property rights, wills and estates, parental roles and duties, counseling, case referral mechanisms, and access to justice. In delivering the intervention, the COMBATs took every opportunity to raise awareness of violence against women and facilitated discussion and reflection on the attitudes and practices that perpetuate it. The program reached 10,755 men and 14,330 women across two intervention districts. In a concluding survey, women from the intervention communities reported a lower number of experiences of violence from their intimate partners than did women from the control communities. Furthermore, women's experiences of sexual violence in the intervention communities were reduced by 55 percent (from 17.1 to 7.7 percent), while the prevalence of physical intimate partner violence was reduced by 50 percent (from 16.5 to 8.3 percent).[8]

Ultimately, community engagement is a critical focus of VAWG prevention programming. Interventions are more likely to be effective in transforming attitudes about VAWG when they are community led, locally owned, and specific to the context in which violence occurs, allowing for the development of trust among stakeholders and greater levels of engagement and commitment by participants.

19

ECONOMICS AND VAWG

What economic factors affect VAWG?

There are many economic factors that affect the incidence and prevalence of VAWG. As discussed in chapter 9, poverty is a key player, along with stable and secure employment and conflict-free societies in which national economies can prosper. With regard to poverty, the relationship is bidirectional. In one direction, poorer women and girls are typically more dependent on male partners and relatives and have less household decision-making power, which aggravates their risk of experiencing violence and lowers their capacity to leave violent or abusive relationships. In the other direction, poverty increases other risk factors of violence for women, including poor health, limited education, low social status, and household economic insecurity and stress. More broadly, women and girls who experience violence at home are also at risk of increased poverty due to the direct and indirect costs of violence, including medical expenses, lost income, and reduced productivity.

Globalized economic cycles of boom and bust often deepen gendered inequalities in societies and escalate risk factors for VAWG. Mortgage foreclosures, austerity policies, and job losses (especially in the public sector, where women are disproportionately employed) all increase financial and psychological stress, which in turn increases drug and alcohol abuse, poverty, and VAWG. Economic globalization processes can also exacerbate VAWG through men's reactions to them and the loss of male entitlement to resources and income that often results. For instance, where neoliberal reforms open economies to global competition, there may be increased opportunities for women to enter the labor market and gain economic independence. Firms in competitive global markets may prefer to hire women rather than men, especially where their labor is deemed cheaper due to prevailing gender structures and ideologies. Yet the obverse of this economic empowerment for women can sometimes be men's economic disempowerment. For instance, a South African study found that in an attempt to maintain their hold on dominant forms of masculinity, men reacted violently to the greater economic opportunities for women and to rising male unemployment.[1] Men's ideas of successful masculinity were linked to their ability to become or remain economic providers for the family. Given this, men facing chronic unemployment described feeling powerless as a justification for violence against women.

Women's economic contributions to the family can also affect their risk of physical and emotional abuse. In a cross-national comparison of the role of economic factors in women's risk of intimate partner violence in Canada and the United States, Kaukinen and Powers (2015) found that employed women were at greater risk of experiencing violence and abuse by an intimate partner than unemployed women. They found that employment has both socioeconomic and symbolic implications for women's decision-making, both of which were likely associated with women's risk for intimate partner violence. Moreover, American women were found to be at an elevated risk for partner violence compared with Canadian women. The researchers attributed this to the greater availability of income-supplementing programs, such as family leave, extensive employment insurance, and social welfare programming in Canada, which likely insulate women from the risk for violence by male intimate partners. Regardless of country, both income and education were found to be insulators to violence by an intimate partner. Higher levels of income and education provide women with an alternative to being financially dependent on an intimate partner and at risk for violence, while offering a clear pathway to leaving a violent relationship.

Rising housing costs in major cities, as well as housing shortages, are also economic factors that can contribute to VAWG. This is because both aspects of housing can push women and girls seeking alternative living arrangements out of the market. In an effort to avoid homelessness, women and girls can place themselves at serious risk by continuing to stay with controlling, violent, or abusive partners or family members. Furthermore, increased demand for homeless services and shelters for women seeking to escape violence can further expose them to harm and prolong their recovery and re-establishment in productive society. The American Civil Liberties Union reported[2] that 46 percent of homeless women in Minnesota said they had previously stayed in abusive relationships because they had nowhere to go, and that in 36 percent of US cities domestic violence was found to be a primary cause of homelessness. Likewise, in Australia in 2015–2016, 38 percent of all people requesting assistance from specialist homelessness agencies reported doing so to escape domestic or family violence (amounting to 106,000 clients), including 31,000 children under age 15 and 66,000 women.[3]

What are the economic costs of VAWG?

In every country and globally, VAWG is an extremely costly problem. In the United States, the cost of violence is estimated to be up to $500 billion per year. In Egypt, 500,000 working days are lost each year due to marital violence.[4] In Australia, the total annual cost of VAWG in 2015–2016 was estimated to be $22 billion AUD.[5] In Vietnam, direct costs of VAWG, such as women's loss of earnings, out-of-pocket expenses, medical costs, police support, legal aid, counseling services, judicial support, and lost school fees, are estimated to be 1.4 percent of its GDP. These examples show that VAWG is incredibly costly to national economies and their resources, and given high levels of nonreporting of VAWG and difficulties in fully capturing the long-term, generational costs of violence in society, these estimates are only conservative.

Violence against women and girls has significant economic costs for individuals and households. These include costs related to healthcare; filing a complaint in a police station or a case in court; and food, accommodation, and replacing damaged property. Furthermore, women and their families feel the impact of violence on their employment, household work, and children's school attendance; all may be abandoned when dealing with the aftereffects of violence. Finally, financial costs of violence place a significant burden on the economic security of households, which is exacerbated in countries experiencing economic uncertainty and/or high levels of poverty. For example, a report on intimate partner violence in South Sudan found that 11 percent of women reported out-of-pocket expenditure as a result of intimate partner violence; in the case of one or more forms of VAWG, 7 percent of women experiencing violence reported incurring expenditures. The study found that women had spent an average of US$21 on VAWG-related expenses in the previous 12 months—a particularly substantial burden given that 80 percent of the population of South Sudan lives on less than US$1 per day.

There are significant economic costs of VAWG for businesses as well. The experience and perpetration of sexual violence affecting female employees, including belittling sexual commentary, inappropriate touching, sexual assault, and rape, has significant consequences for business output and productivity. Women who face such violence may be later to or absent from work as a result of it or, alternatively, may engage in presenteeism to avoid violent predatory situations at home or away from work. Finally, VAWG may serve as a distraction at or from work, leading to reduced productivity. In Ghana, one in four female employees in the surveyed businesses reported productivity loss as a result of violence in the previous 12 months, equivalent to 14 working days for each employee affected. Overall, the national loss in productivity in Ghana through missing work and/or lowered productivity at work due to VAWG is equivalent to 65 million days annually, which is equal to 4.5 percent of employed women not working.[6]

What are other economic consequences of VAWG?

The economic consequences of VAWG are wide-reaching. Beyond their impact on personal household economies and the wider labor force, the effects can be felt in more indirect ways; for instance, in the form of intergenerational economic harm to the children of victims, the impact on a woman's capacity to undertake care work, and clear costs to the community in its provision of healthcare and access to justice to victims of VAWG.

Violence against women and girls can have significant intergenerational impacts. For instance, if children consistently miss school as a result of VAWG, this can result in reduced capabilities in the long term, such as an impact on the child's future earnings, as well as the potential for families to lose the return on their investment in children's education. Indeed, missed school days represent an important loss of investment by households, particularly in places where education is more inaccessible and expensive relative to income.

Another dimension of lost productivity as a result of VAWG is its impact on care work, which includes work that women do in addition to home-based production activities. Care work is an important cost of VAWG that, while usually invisible in national economic models, has become increasingly recognized as contributing considerably to the overall output of an economy. The ability to perform care work may be impeded by physical injuries that result from violence, as well as anxiety, depression, and debilitating stress. Often, a woman's inability to perform care work results in that burden being shifted to another family member, usually a daughter or other female family member, reflecting the gendered intergenerational consequences of VAWG. For example, due to experiences of violence within and outside the home, women survivors in Pakistan were unable to undertake care work for the equivalent of approximately 11 million days in 2018–2019.

Economic consequences of VAWG for the wider community include effects on the provision of healthcare and justice. The cost of healthcare services consumed as a result of domestic violence (including emergency room and clinic visits, hospital stays, mental health services, medication, and physical therapy) is one of the most significant cost components of VAWG. It also has economic consequences for the justice system (in relation to the resources expended in civil, criminal, and administrative structures) and the provision of social services (shelters, income support, and other support services) for women and their children. UN Women estimated that the total average costs of accessing healthcare—namely, the cost of the service, cost of transportation, and medical costs incurred per incident—for survivors of VAWG in Vietnam was 804,000 VND per incident (approx. US$35), which amounted to 28 percent of women's average monthly income in 2013 (see Duvvury and colleagues 2012). This makes visible the economic burden of VAWG on both the individual and the surrounding community, which may lack the requisite resources to deal appropriately and comprehensively with situations of violence.

Can women's economic empowerment prevent or reduce VAWG?

Women's economic empowerment has a number of direct and flow-on effects that can help to prevent VAWG. Specifically, improvement in the economic status of women is likely to offer women opportunities and resources to both prevent and to leave violent relationships. It is often the case that the further removed women are from paid labor, the less power they exert in their relationships. This is because women's economic independence from male partners typically results in greater decision-making power within relationships and households, which can translate to greater power and control in determining future activity. Furthermore, stable employment can help to mold women's routines away from home, expanding their social networks and reducing the isolation and dependency that would otherwise increase their vulnerability to violence.

However, at the same time, women's economic empowerment also has the potential to exacerbate VAWG. Some men may interpret women's employment as a threat to their leading family role and breadwinner status. This is particularly the case where female employment is less normative or occurs at the start of women's transition into a given labor force. Thus, a woman's risk of violence would be higher when her improved social status from employment and economic empowerment is treated as threatening traditional gender norms and social hierarchies. That being said, following the normalization of women's employment over time, economic independence can serve as a tool for women to protect themselves from violence. Fruitful research has been conducted into interventions that pair economic empowerment and gender-transformative education, as discussed in chapter 18. Importantly, these interventions provide a platform to engage poor men on gender equality and VAWG so as to prevent a backlash against women and girls following their economic empowerment.

For example, Sammanit Jeevan was a family-centered economic empowerment intervention designed to prevent VAWG in migrant communities in Baglung District, Nepal.[7] It worked with young married women, their husbands, mothers-in-law, and fathers-in-law, who often all lived together. The intervention was based on 20 three-hour participatory sessions, and materials that cost U$150 were provided to families for income-generating activities. The program was successful in improving both the livelihoods, savings, and domestic relations between young married women, their husbands, and their in-laws. Women reported having more control over their earnings and greater recognition of their economic value in the family. Furthermore, both women and men reported fewer patriarchal gender attitudes, and women also perceived that wider community social norms became significantly less patriarchal after intervention. Women's experiences of physical violence in their relationships were also reduced from 10 to 4 percent.

Have government austerity and financial recession affected the responses to VAWG?

Government austerity and financial recession can have a significant effect on both the prevalence and incidence of VAWG, as well as on state responses to VAWG. The consequences of economic reform and tightened government budgets may not be immediately visible but are concealed in the quiet transformation of households hit by foreclosures, loss of income, youth unemployment, and out-of-work men. These social and economic changes represent risk factors for domestic and family violence, in which women and children are frequently made targets.

However, increased violence, alcoholism, depression, and suicide should not be treated as the inevitable effects of economic downturns; rather, they should be seen as arising out of the political choices of governments. To the extent that recessions disenfranchise populations and worsen economic security, employment prospects, and the financial stress of individuals and families, in combination with what is known about the determinants of violent crime (including men's violence against women), it can in fact be expected that VAWG will increase in such circumstances if other mitigating measures are not established.

To take this point further, austerity measures are rarely neutral in their effect; often, they impact the provision of social services, which has direct consequences for VAWG. In relation to domestic violence, for instance, this impact is seen through a variety of avenues—cuts to police and criminal justice funding for anti-VAWG measures; removal of government funding for charities working on domestic violence; and wider cuts to social services, including those related to homelessness, healthcare, and education—that structurally contribute to the rise of VAWG. These economic choices exacerbate known contributing factors to VAWG and simultaneously result in the shrinking of services available to those at risk or experiencing VAWG. For example, in the United Kingdom, Trades Union Congress and Women's Aid investigated financial abuse in the context of the disproportionate impacts of recession and austerity on women, and specifically, the creation of universal credit, a single integrated monthly household welfare payment.[8] The findings show how paying benefit claims online to accounts accessible to perpetrators of VAWG exacerbated problems of financial control and exploitation of women, thereby demonstrating the potential negative impacts of the reformed payment system on the safety and security of domestic violence victims.

Economic crises are known to impact family dynamics due to household stress and conditions that exacerbate unemployment, income stagnation or loss, and economic hardship. Sharp economic downturns can increase abusive behavior in two ways. First, job loss and material hardship can increase VAWG, in the sense that spouses who might not have otherwise expressed violence while economic outlooks were positive may adopt abusive behaviors as a result of the stress of challenging economic circumstances. Second, worsening macroeconomic conditions result in greater fear and uncertainty throughout society, and this loss of control over economic circumstances may result in greater efforts to control a different area of one's life, such as intimate and/or family relationships. Schneider and colleagues (2016) tested this idea by examining the relationship between mothers' experiences of domestic violence and adverse labor market conditions in the lead-up to and occurrence of the global financial crisis (2001–2010). They found that unemployment and economic hardship at the household level were associated with increased abusive behavior. In addition, sharp increases in the overall unemployment rate increased men's controlling behavior toward intimate partners, regardless of the impact of unemployment and economic distress on their particular households. This study and others show that the anticipatory anxiety that frequently accompanies sudden economic downturns has clear negative effects on household gender relations, over and above the effects of job loss and material hardship, which can exacerbate the risk of VAWG.

20

ADVOCACY FRAMEWORKS

ENDING VAWG

What theories of social and behavioral change inform current advocacy to end VAWG?

Prevention of VAWG requires deep societal transformation in norms, structures, and institutions. Such transformation can only occur when a critical mass of people can no longer tolerate the status quo and come together to create meaningful, lasting change. A theory of change explains how initial and seemingly small-scale accomplishments can preempt the achievement of long-range positive outcomes; in other words, a theory of change helps us navigate the actions (and their underlying core principles) required for lasting social change. We cannot create change alone; we need to work with others, including those who may seem resistant, to build a movement to prevent violence. To do so, we need to identify and address the root causes of VAWG. We also need different anti-VAWG approaches working at different levels in different time frames that can reinforce each other to maximize the chances of reducing and preventing violence. Finally, we need to continually check and scrutinize our approaches by asking: Are these methods working? For whom? How?

Many advocacy organizations have their own theories of change to combat VAWG. Ideally, such theories complement government action in the implementation of laws, policies, and services to effect change. For example, ActionAid is a global organization working with women and girls to end violence and fight poverty.[1] Its theory of change on ending gender-based VAWG is underpinned by a number of key principles, three of which are worth highlighting. First, women's rights organizations create and sustain change, especially those working to tackle VAWG, in order to make change and build strong and inclusive social movements. Second, empowering women is both the means and the end; focusing on the rights of, and being accountable to, women and girls is the most effective way of tackling gender inequality as the root cause of VAWG. Third, backlash is inevitable but manageable; resistance to tackling VAWG, which may include increased risk of further violence, will occur where root causes are being addressed, but this can be managed. By using these principles as a guiding force on action against gender-based violence, ActionAid ensures that their advocacy is sustainable, victim-focused, and transformative across different cultures, contexts, and societies.

Furthermore, the framing of VAWG as a threat to public health has been crucial to the theory of change informing advocacy frameworks. Public health approaches aim to prevent problems from occurring in the first place by targeting key risk factors or social determinants and addressing these across entire populations, not just in limited contexts or social groups. Public health approaches were originally designed for disease prevention but have been successfully modified to apply to anti-VAWG advocacy. Specifically, the public health model acknowledges that the effects of VAWG extend beyond private and criminal justice spheres given its marked impact on physical and mental health, social well-being, and other aspects of social needs. This advocacy mindset has created new opportunities for the health sector to be involved in guiding prevention work, therefore reducing dependence on criminal justice mechanisms and other services. Within the public health approach, primary prevention of VAWG incorporates any program, policy, campaign, or other measure that seeks to address underlying factors of VAWG and reduce its likelihood of occurring. As mentioned throughout this book, these measures may include programs and strategies to promote respectful and gender-equitable relationships, nonviolent social and cultural norms, and greater access to material resources and support systems for both potential victims and perpetrators.

Lori Heise's ecological explanation of a public health approach suggests that ubiquitous male dominance and gender inequality provide an important yet incomplete explanation of VAWG.[2] Specifically, Heise suggests that it is necessary to incorporate other social and individual factors to explain why it is that despite all men having exposure to cultural messages of superiority and power, only some of them perpetrate violence. The political economy of VAWG complements the ecological model by further taking into account the globalized structures of war and economic competition in the pressures exacerbating and compounding VAWG. It explains that while women as a group are disproportionately targeted by men's violence, some women are more vulnerable than others, and some men are more likely to be perpetrators because of the effects of globalized economic and neocolonial structures that reflect transnational race, ethnic, and class inequalities. In this sense, both a public health approach and a political economy explanation acknowledge the interrelatedness of different spheres of social life (personal, communal, societal) and the interactions between individuals and their environments. This allows both approaches to take into account the multiple and intersecting causes of VAWG in their advocacy and pursuit of a theory of change that targets these complex dimensions across whole populations.

Do social norms and marketing campaigns change behavior and attitudes toward VAWG?

Challenging cultural and social norms supportive of VAWG can help reduce and prevent violent behavior. A social norms approach to behavior change assumes that people often hold mistaken ideas about the attitudes and behavior of others— that is, that individuals overestimate the prevalence of risky behaviors and underestimate the prevalence of protective behaviors. This misjudgment results in a greater level of justification and higher prevalence of risky behaviors in an individual, as well as an increased likelihood that any discomfort that ensues from such behaviors will be kept silent. The social norms approach seeks to revise these misperceptions among individuals by giving them a more realistic sense of actual behaviors. For example, to reduce women's experiences of sexual assault and increase understanding of noncoercive sexual behavior norms, the A Man Respects a Woman project based in Washington State adopted a social norms marketing campaign intended for university-age men, as well as male peer education and a theater presentation. An evaluation conducted two years later found that the men involved had become more accurate in their perceptions of other men's behavior; fewer men accepted that the average male student has sex with drunk partners, and they reported more positive behavior and attitudes toward seeking and responding to consent and nonconsent.

Social marketing uses marketing principles and techniques to impact individuals within their social environments. It operates as a planned, long-term approach to changing human behavior through segmentation, targeting, and awareness of competing norms and attitudes. Social marketing campaigns can change attitudes and behavior related to VAWG by combining interventions across different levels. As discussed previously, VAWG is complex and influenced by individual, family, community, society, and global factors. To effect change, a multisectoral approach is required, with several interventions and programs reinforcing each other to produce a gradual and sustainable process of change.

Gender-transformative social marketing programs working on multiple levels—for instance, media campaigns, community activities, VAWG-responsive policy and services, and structural changes that promote gender equality—have the potential to produce positive change in VAWG. For example, New Zealand's Family Violence: It's Not Okay campaign (2007) produced some constructive outcomes. It operated as a community awareness campaign targeting male perpetrators to increase the understanding of domestic and family violence and reduce violent tendencies. The campaign involved TV advertisements, videos, a telephone helpline, posters, community action toolkits, local government and business engagement, and research and evaluation programs. Upon evaluation in November 2008, the New Zealand government measured campaign awareness at 95 percent, with almost one in four people reporting that their views on family violence had changed as a result of the campaign.[3] Further review in 2015 found that the campaign had led to increased awareness of family violence, an increase in family violence reports to police, lower personal thresholds to report, and a greater sense of community ownership regarding family violence.[4]

Similarly, the Welsh Government's Live Fear Free social marketing campaign seeks to create dialogue about domestic violence and violence against women generally. It has included a Don't Be a Bystander campaign (2018) in film, radio, digital, and social media formats, which received extensive media coverage and resulted in a doubling of calls from concerned others to the VAWG helpline compared to the previous year. The associated This Is Me campaign (2018) was aimed at addressing how conformity with gender inequality can be a cause and consequence of VAWG, and it was applied through a multimedia campaign across broadcast, outdoor, and digital channels, including a "selfie board" on social media and several case studies. While the relative newness of Live Fear Free makes it difficult to judge its impact, its similarity to the New Zealand campaign suggests that social marketing regarding VAWG can be effective in increasing the reach and awareness of the problem. Specifically, by creating a public that is willing to change its behavior and attitudes and is receptive to more effective community interventions working with survivors and perpetrators, activism and advocacy about VAWG can increase, thereby encouraging the development of more responsive VAWG laws and policies, as well as better-funded public services to protect survivors.

What have been the impacts of national and international activist campaigns such as the 16 Days of Activism against Gender-Based Violence?

All strong social movements have the capacity to shape public and government agendas, create the political will to address societal problems, and encourage impactful institutional reforms. In this sense, national antiviolence activists are no different; just like other social campaigners, they lobby; protest; make submissions to government; hold conferences; and establish connections that bring them into contact with key policy influencers, such as government officials, business leaders, and community personalities. However, what is particularly powerful about anti-VAWG campaigns and feminist activism more generally is their ability to model new forms of social organization, including through publications (e.g., newsletters, bulletins), research, charity partnerships, and cultural events, such as the 16 Days of Activism against Gender-Based Violence.

In fact, it has been argued that this broader undercurrent of change is critically important because it conditions lobbyists and other state actors who, while seeming more influential, require the background support of the feminist movement to effect meaningful change. For instance, Weldon and Htun (2013) examined 70 countries over four decades (1975–2005) to identify the factors associated with progressive state action to combat VAWG. Their analysis revealed that the presence of a strong, autonomous feminist movement was a key predictor of government action targeting VAWG. Countries with stronger feminist movements were found to have more comprehensive policies on VAWG, more impetus toward legal reform, and greater funding for VAWG services than those countries with weaker or nonexistent movements.

Effective movements work transnationally and demand the creation of new institutions in different settings and societies in which to embed ideas and advance feminist interests. In this sense, international activist campaigns can create domestic pressure and induce change. For example, the Victorian Law Reform Commission in Australia has acknowledged the role of women's movements in shaping its recommendations for reform of state sexual assault laws.[5] These recommendations, which challenged stereotypes about sexual behavior and discriminatory attitudes toward women and children contained in the previous law, were a key driver in the introduction of new legislation for sexual offenses. Furthermore, many of the judicial, community, and service-based recommendations in the Commission's report advocated for by women's groups, such as establishment of police multidisciplinary centers, child witness services, specialist prosecutors, and sexual assault forensic nurses, were then implemented by the Victorian government.

Feminist activism has also shaped VAWG policies through transnational advocacy. Specifically, transnational antiviolence movements create pressure on governments by pushing for the adoption of international standards to eliminate VAWG. According to Weldon and Htun (2013), this can happen in three main ways. The first is through the state reporting mechanisms of global treaties on women's rights and human rights such as CEDAW, the Beijing Platform for Action, and the UN Human Right's Council's Periodic Review of Human Rights, all of which specifically address VAWG. This is because the signing of these instruments raises expectations and mobilizes populations and nonstate actors (e.g., NGOs) to hold their governments to account on their global commitments. Second, regional agreements on VAWG can influence governments.

For example, the Organization of American States' (OAS) *Inter-American Convention on Violence Against Women* (1994) was a leading regional agreement that helped to strengthen international antiviolence norms by emphasizing the different way these norms applied to specific states, thereby encouraging more nuanced regional adoption and action. Third, as successful anti-VAWG norms and movements spread across regions and even globally, they tend to be emulated regardless of differences in the types of regimes and histories of violence between countries.

This latter transnational change mechanism has been deliberately promoted by feminist movements, with 16 Days of Activism against Gender-Based Violence serving as a perfect example. The Centre for Women's Global Leadership has been a leader of anti-VAWG campaigning and the main coordinator of the 16 Days Campaign, deciding on a particular area of anti-VAWG activism to be addressed each year. In 2018 the global advocacy theme was ending gender-based violence and harassment in the world of work. Joined by women's movements around the world as well as the United Nations UNiTE to End Violence against Women Campaign, the movement contributed to the successful adoption of ILO Convention 190 and Recommendation 206 in 2019, a watershed moment in the struggle to eliminate VAWG in the workplace.

Which NGOs and local and transnational movements have had an impact on reducing VAWG in particular contexts?

A plethora of NGO-led, local, and transnational movements have successfully made inroads in reducing VAWG. This is because the pervasive and systemic nature of VAWG allows activism across a variety of contexts. One pertinent example is Ni Una Menos (Not One Less), an antiviolence advocacy coalition across Latin America involving women of all ages, congresswomen, lawyers, and grassroots activists.

Ni Una Menos began in Argentina in 2015 and is dedicated to fighting gender inequality and the abuse and murder of women. The movement was sparked by the murder in 2015 of 14-year-old Chiara Páez, who was found buried in the garden of her 16-year-old boyfriend's house. According to autopsy results, she was pregnant and had been beaten to death. Following this, a tweet by journalist Marcela Ojeda, which read, "Actresses, politicians, artists, businesswomen, opinion makers . . . women, all, . . . aren't we going to speak up? THEY ARE KILLING US," and the resulting hashtag #NiUnaMenos went viral, catalyzing the movement to action. Shortly afterward, a 200,000-strong march led by women journalists and activists took place in front of the Argentine National Congress in Buenos Aires. Activists argued that that murder reflected not only high rates of violence, social conflict, and organized crime in Argentina, but also the cultural strain of aggressive hypermasculinity that was victimizing women and girls.

Ni Una Menos was nothing short of explosive, and the movement quickly spread across Latin America. On its one-year anniversary in 2016, another march took place throughout Argentina's most important cities under a new slogan, #VivasNosQueremos (We Want Us Alive), which was replicated in marches in Montevideo, Uruguay, and Santiago, Chile. A nationwide strike in Argentina was organized following another egregious rape and murder, with street demonstrations arising in Chile, Peru, Bolivia, Paraguay, Uruguay, El Salvador, Guatemala, Mexico, and Spain. In 2018, Ni Una Menos was responsible for one of the largest mobilizations in Argentine history (roughly two million people in Buenos Aires alone) on the occasion of the congressional discussion of a law concerning legal, secure, and free abortion. In 2019 the movement incorporated into its ambit activism on economic crises and called for women's rights to economic security and abortion.

The impact of Ni Una Menos on the visibility of femicide and gender-related violence in Latin America has been significant. The campaign has inspired debate on women's issues that were previously taboo, including domestic violence, sexual assault, abortion, and street harassment. Reporting of VAWG increased by 25 percent in the first six months of activism, and the campaign has resulted in some high-profile prosecutions.[6] Furthermore, the Ni Una Menos movement led to meaningful congressional discussions on safe abortion in Argentina, and although the vote was lost, the bill came closer to passing than ever before. The incredible momentum of Ni Una Menos in just four years demonstrates the potency and potential of meaningful collective activism that all NGOs and local and transnational movements hold, as well as their capacity to have a genuine and lasting impact on VAWG awareness, reduction, and prevention.

What are the shortcomings of current advocacy given that VAWG is persistent and increasing in many contexts?

Not all antiviolence activism is perfect. While current antiviolence strategies may provide temporary affirmative solutions to reducing violence, they may fail to address the structural causes that underpin VAWG, which is necessary to achieve long-term change. While this is not necessarily a shortcoming given that an integrated approach tackling both causes and symptoms of violence is important, focusing only on solutions that address the symptoms of violence may prolong the risk of violence in a given community.

Bicycle initiatives to prevent VAWG in the Global South illustrate this point. While bicycles offer a different means of transportation to alleviate the problem of violence faced by women and girls who walk long distances to school or work, they ultimately fail to address its root causes, thereby stopping short of truly transformative change. For instance, SchoolCycle, launched in 2014 by GirlUp, aims to provide bicycles to girls in disadvantaged countries to help them access education and stay in school. In Malawi, where less than a quarter of girls finish primary school and only 9 percent graduate from secondary school (partly due to distance), GirlUp provided 550 bicycles to girls in two villages, resulting in a 21.4 percent improvement in girls' school attendance by the end of 2015.[7]

This initiative and others like it, however, fail to address the risk of violence for girls within school environments, as detailed in chapter 13. For instance, research in Malawi highlights the pervasive assault of girls by both fellow pupils and teachers while at school. Likewise, this approach seems to neglect the fact that poverty (rather than transportation) is a major factor preventing girls from staying in school, because public schools cost money and require resources that poorer families may be unable to provide. Indeed, women's experiences of physical VAWG increased from 28 percent in 2010 to 34 percent in Malawi's 2015–2016 Demographic and Health Survey.[8] While this increase does not discredit the important work of SchoolCycle and other targeted programs, it does reinforce the need for anti-VAWG programming to tackle root causes, such as the social and cultural norms that condone violence and the culture of impunity around VAWG in Malawi.

Another obvious shortcoming of—or rather, challenge for—anti-VAWG advocacy is maintaining ongoing funding. This is particularly problematic when NGOs are reliant on funding by governments, whose political commitments to addressing VAWG may fluctuate. For instance, in 2010 the Canadian government cut millions of dollars in funding for the continuation of the Sisters in Spirit project, which focused on violence against indigenous women in the justice sector.[9] Likewise, in December 2019 the Australian government axed funding to the National Family Violence Prevention and Legal Services Forum, a civil society body representing indigenous survivors of domestic violence in Australia.[10]

There are many examples of similar retrenchment within and across other countries around the world, indicating that anti-VAWG advocacy is often not supported inclusively, thus failing to protect those who may be the most marginalized and at risk of violence. This is often due to the intersecting levels of discrimination and risk that women and girls face as a result of their age, culture, social status, ethnicity, religion, and so on. Indeed, consider the previously mentioned cuts in light of the fact that indigenous women in Canada are three times more likely to be killed by a stranger than non-Aboriginal women,[11] and in Australia, they are 31 times more likely to be hospitalized due to domestic violence than non-indigenous women and girls.[12] Advocacy and anti-VAWG programming that intentionally or unintentionally excludes certain subsets of a population from receiving the benefit of protection can counteract other proactive efforts for violence prevention.

NOTES

Chapter 1

1. Mamoun, Abdelhak. 2014. "EXCLUSIVE: ISIS document sets prices of Christian and Yazidi slaves." *Iraqi News*, November 3.
2. Sanders, Katie. 2014. "Steinem: More women killed by partners since 9/11 than deaths from attacks, ensuing wars." *PunditFact*, October 7. https://www.politifact.com/punditfact/statements/2014/oct/07/gloria-steinem/steinem-more-women-killed-partners-911-deaths-atta/.
3. Jones, Samuel. 2015. "Ending bacha bazi: Boy sex slavery and the responsibility to protect doctrine." *Indiana International Comparative Law Review* 25, no. 1: 63–78.
4. For further accessible commentary on male victims of gender-based violence, see Hamilton, Rob. 2019. "'Hidden traumas'— when men are victims of gender-based and sexual violence." *Gender Justice*, February 5. https://www.justgender.org/hidden-traumas-when-men-are-victims-of-gender-based-and-sexual-violence/.

Chapter 2

1. For further discussion of this scandal and many others, see Dyhouse, Carol. 2013. *Girl trouble: Panic and progress in the history of young women*. London: Zed Books.
2. Rowbotham, Sheila. 1979. *Beyond the fragments: Feminism and the making of socialism*. London: Merlin.
3. Goodmark, Leigh. 2018. *Decriminalizing domestic violence: A balanced policy approach to intimate partner violence*. Berkeley: University of California Press.

4. Guest, Carly. 2016. "The memory-work group: Feminist belonging." In *Becoming feminist: Narratives and memories*. London: Palgrave Macmillan UK.
5. Amos, Valerie, and Pratibha Pramar. 1984. "Challenging imperial feminism." *Feminist Review* 17: 3–19.
6. Roche, Susan E., Katy Biron, and Niamh Reilly. 1995. "Sixteen days of activism against gender violence." *Violence Against Women* 1, no. 3: 272–81.

Chapter 3
1. World Health Organisation. 2013. *Global and regional estimates of violence against women: Prevalence and health effects of intimate partner violence and non-partner sexual violence*. Geneva: WHO.
2. Amaral, Sofia, Sonia Bhalotraz, and Nishith Prakash. 2019. *Gender, crime and punishment: Evidence from women police stations in India*. IDEAS Working Paper Series. St. Louis, MO: RePEc.
3. ANROWS. 2014. *Fast facts: Indigenous family violence*. Sydney: ANROWS. https://www.anrows.org.au/media-releases/indigenous-family-violence/.
RAINN. 2020. *Victims of Sexual Violence Statistics*. https://www.rainn.org/statistics/victims-sexual-violence.
Note that the RAINN statistics were generated using data from the following source: Bureau of Justice Statistics. 2014. *Crimes Against the Elderly, 2003–2013*. Washington, DC: US Department of Justice. https://www.bjs.gov/content/pub/pdf/cae0313.pdf
UN-Habitat. 2013. *State of Women in Cities 2012–2013: Gender and the Prosperity of Cities*. Nairobi: UN-Habitat.
4. UN Trust Fund to End Violence against Women. 2017. *Fact sheet: Ending violence against women and girls with disabilities*. New York: UN Women. https://untf.unwomen.org/en/digital-library/publications/2017/08/ending-violence-against-women-and-girls-with-disabilities
Marques Garcia, Luana, Diana Ortiz and Anne-Marie Urban. 2019. *Violence against Women and Girls with Disabilities: Latin America and the Caribbean*. Policy Brief. Washington, DC: Inter-American Development Bank. https://publications.iadb.org/en/violence-against-women-and-girls-disabilities-latin-america-and-caribbean

Humanity & Inclusion. 2018. *Gender and disability intersectionality in practice: Women and girls with disabilities addressing discrimination and violence in Africa.* Lyon: Humanity & Inclusion. https://admin.makingitwork-crpd.org/sites/default/files/2018-06/MIW_GenderAndDisability_Report-June2018.pdf

5. Amaral, Sofia, Sonia Bhalotraz and Nishith Prakash. 2019. *Gender, Crime and Punishment: Evidence from Women Police Stations in India.* IDEAS Working Paper Series. St Louis: RePEc. https://ideas.repec.org/p/bos/iedwpr/dp-309.html

6. UN Women. 2019. "Services for all women." In *What we do: Ending violence against women.* https://www.unwomen.org/en/what-we-do/ending-violence-against-women/services-for-all-women.

7. Poll: Thomson Reuters Foundation. 2011. "The world's most dangerous countries for women 2011–POLL." https://news.trust.org/spotlight/the-worlds-most-dangerous-countries-for-women-2011 Survey: Re Bogota: Thomson Reuters Foundation. 2014. "Most dangerous transport systems for women." https://news.trust.org/spotlight/most-dangerous-transport-systems-for-women/.
Re India: Thomson Reuters Foundation. 2012. "G20 countries: the worst and best for women." https://news.trust.org/spotlight/g20-countries-the-worst-and-best-for-women/

8. Thomson Reuters Foundation. 2018. "The World's Most Dangerous Countries for Women." Annual Poll. https://poll2018.trust.org/.

Chapter 4

1. Janine Mouzos and Toni Makkai. 2004. *Women's experiences of male violence: findings from the Australian Component of the International Violence against Women Survey (IVAWS).* Australian Institute of Criminology.

2. National Institute of Population Research and Training—NIPORT/Bangladesh, Mitra and Associates/Bangladesh, and ORC Macro. 2005. *Bangladesh Demographic and Health Survey 2004.* Dhaka, Bangladesh: National Institute of Population Research and Training, Mitra and Associates, and ORC Macro.

3. Tausch, Arno. 2019. "Multivariate analyses of the global acceptability rates of male intimate partner violence (IPV) against women based on World Values Survey data." *International Journal of Health Planning and Management* 34, no. 4: 1155–94.

4. Mitchell, Juliet. 1971. *Women's estate*. New York: Vintage Books.

5. UN News. 2018. "Increasingly under attack, women human rights defenders need better back up." *UN News*, November 28.

6. UN News. 2020. "Colombia: Staggering number of human rights defenders killed in 2019." *UN News*, January 14. https://news.un.org/en/story/2020/01/1055272

7. Anderson, Stephanie. 2016. "Julia Gillard says women going into politics should expect rape threats." *ABC News*, October 12.

Chapter 5

1. The Asia Foundation. 2017. *The state of conflict and violence in Asia*. San Francisco, CA: The Asia Foundation.

2. Awori, Thelma, Catherine Lutz, and Paban Thapa. 2013. *Final report: Expert mission to evaluate risks to SEA prevention*. New York: United Nations.

Chapter 6

1. Brown, Thea, Danielle Tyson, and Paula Fernandez Arias. 2014. "Filicide and parental separation and divorce." *Child Abuse Review* 23, no 2: 75–78.

2. Bloom, Mia 2011. "Bombshells: Women and Terror." *Gender Issues* 28: 15

3. Brown, Sara E. 2013. "Female perpetrators of the Rwandan genocide." *International Feminist Journal of Politics* 16, no 3: 448–69.

4. Féron, Élise. 2018. *Wartime sexual violence against men: Masculinities and power in conflict zones*. : Rowman & Littlefield International.

Chapter 7

1. Rao, Arati. 1995. "The Politics of Gender and Culture in International Human Rights Discourse." In *Women's Rights, Human Rights: International Feminist Perspectives*, ed. Julie Peters and Andrea Wolper. New York: Routledge.

2. Ministry of Health and Population (Egypt), El-Zanaty and Associates (Egypt), and ICF International. 2015. *Egypt health issues survey 2015*. Cairo, Egypt, and Rockville, MD: Ministry of Health and Population and ICF International.

3. UN Commission on Human Rights. 2000. *Extrajudicial, summary or arbitrary executions: report of the Special Rapporteur, Asma Jahangir, submitted pursuant to Commission on Human Rights resolution 1999/35.* UN Doc E/CN.4/2000/3, January 25.

4. National Population Commission (NPC) and ICF International. 2014. *Nigeria Demographic and Health Survey 2013.* Abuja, Nigeria and Rockville, MD: NPC and ICF International. https://dhsprogram.com/pubs/pdf/FR293/FR293.pdf.

Chapter 8

1. Stankiewicz, J. M., and F. Rosselli. 2008. "Women as sex objects and victims in print advertisements." *Sex Roles: A Journal of Research* 58, nos. 7–8: 579–89.

2. Farrow, Ronan. 2017. "From aggressive overtures to sexual assault: Harvey Weinstein's accusers tell their stories." *New Yorker*, October 10.

3. Office of the eSafety Commissioner (Australia). 2017. *Image-based abuse: Qualitative research summary.* Canberra, ACT: Office of the eSafety Commissioner.

4. Henry, Nicola, Asher Flynn, and Anastasia Powell. 2019. *Responding to "revenge pornography": Prevalence, nature and impacts.* Report to the Criminology Research Advisory Council. Canberra: Australian Institute of Criminology.

5. Usdin, S. 1999. "Soul City takes on AIDS and violence against women." *Aids Bulletin* 8, no. 3: 28–30.

Chapter 9

1. World Health Organization. 2013. *Global and regional estimates of violence against women prevalence and health effects of intimate partner violence and non-partner sexual violence.* Geneva: WHO.

2. International Center for Research on Women. 2009. *Intimate Partner Violence: High Costs to Households and Communities.* Washington, DC: International Center for Research on Women. https://www.icrw.org/wp-content/uploads/2016/10/Intimate-Partner-Violence-High-Cost-to-Households-and-Communities.pdf
Duvvury, Nata, Nguyen Huu Minh and Patricia Carney. 2012. *Estimating the Cost of Domestic Violence against Women in Viet Nam.* Hanoi: UN Women. https://www.unwomen.org/en/digital-library/publications/2013/2/estimating-the-cost-of-domestic-violence-against-women-in-viet-nam

3. Amaral, S., S. Bandyopadhyay, and R. Sensarma. 2015. *Public Work Programs and Gender-based Violence: The Case of NREGA in India*. Discussion Paper 15-09, Department of Economics, Birmingham University.

4. Paul, Sohini. 2016. "Women's labour force participation and domestic violence: Evidence from India." *Journal of South Asian Development* 11, no. 2: 224–50.

5. Gage, A. J., and N. J. Thomas. 2017. "Women's work, gender roles, and intimate partner violence in Nigeria." *Archives of Sexual Behavior* 46, no. 7: 1923–38.

6. Duvvury, Nata, Nguyen Huu Minh, and Patricia Carney. 2012. *Estimating the cost of domestic violence against women in Viet Nam*. Hanoi: UN Women.

7. Vyas, Seema. 2013. *Estimating the association between women's earnings and partner violence: Evidence from the 2008–2009 Tanzania national panel survey*. Women's Voice, Agency, and Participation Research Series (no. 2). Washington, DC: World Bank.

8. Morrison, Andrew R., and Man'a Beatriz Orlando. 1999. "Social and economic costs of domestic violence: Chile and Nicaragua." In *Too close to home: Domestic violence in the Americas*, ed. Andrew R. Morrison and María Loreto Biehl. New York: Inter-American Development Bank, 51–67.

9. KPMG. 2017. *Too costly to ignore: The economic impact of gender-based violence in South Africa*. South Africa: KPMG Human and Social Services.

10. KPMG. 2016. *The cost of violence against women and their children in Australia: Final report for the Department of Social Services*. Canberra, Australia: KPMG Human and Social Services.

11. Agarwal, B., and P. Panda. 2007. "Toward freedom from domestic violence: The neglected obvious." *Journal of Human Development* 8, no. 3: 359–88.

12. The International Women's Human Rights Clinic. 2009. "Women's land and property rights in Kenya—moving forward into a new era of equality: A human rights report and proposed legislation." *Georgetown Journal of International Law* 40: 1–126.

13. Oduro, Abena D., Carmen Diana Deere, and Zachary B. Catanzarite. 2015. "Women's wealth and intimate partner violence: Insights from Ecuador and Ghana." *Feminist Economics* 21, no. 2: 1–29.

14. Ismayilova, L. 2015. "Spousal violence in 5 transitional countries: A population-based multilevel analysis of individual and contextual factors." *American Journal of Public Health* 105, no. 11: 12–22.

15. Yitbarek K., M. Woldie, and G. Abraham. 2019. "Time for action: Intimate partner violence troubles one third of Ethiopian women." *PLoS ONE* 14, no. 5: e0216962.

16. Khalid, J., and M. T. Choudhry. 2018. "Violence and economic empowerment of women in Pakistan: An empirical investigation." *Journal of Interpersonal Violence:* 1–16. Sep:886260518800318. doi: 10.1177/0886260518800318.

17. Bamiwuye, S. O., and C. Odimegwu. 2014. "Spousal violence in sub-Saharan Africa: Does household poverty-wealth matter?" *Reproductive Health* 11, no. 45: 1–10.

18. Gupta, Jhumka, Kathryn L. Falb, Heidi Lehmann, Denise Kpebo, Ziming Xuan, Mazeda Hossain, Cathy Zimmerman, Charlotte Watts, and Jeannie Annan. 2013. "Gender norms and economic empowerment intervention to reduce intimate partner violence against women in rural Côte d'Ivoire: A randomized controlled pilot study." *BMC International Health and Human Rights* 13, no. 46: 1–12.

19. Ranganathan, Meghna, Louise Knight, Tanya Abramsky, Lufuno Muvhango, Tara Polzer Ngwato, Mpho Mbobelatsi, Giulia Ferrari, Charlotte Watts, and Heidi Stöckl. 2019. "Associations between women's economic and social empowerment and intimate partner violence: Findings from a microfinance plus program in rural North West Province, South Africa." *Journal of Interpersonal Violence*: 1–29. https://doi.org/10.1177/0886260519836952.

20. Bandiera, Oriana, Niklas Buehren, Robin Burgess, Markus Goldstein, Selim Gulesci, Imran Rasul, and Munshi Sulaiman. *Empowering adolescent girls: Evidence from a randomized control trial in Uganda.* enGender Impact: The World Bank's Gender Impact Evaluation Database. Washington, DC: World Bank.

21. Raj, Anita, Jay G. Silverman, Jeni Klugman, Niranjan Saggurti, Balaiah Dontad, and Holly B. Shakya. 2018. "Longitudinal analysis of the impact of economic empowerment on risk for intimate partner violence among married women in rural Maharashtra, India." *Social Science & Medicine* 196: 197–203.

Chapter 10

1. Sisters for Change. 2016. *Eliminating violence against women at work: Making sexual harassment laws real for Karnataka's women garment workers*. London: Sisters for Change.
2. Equality and Human Rights Commission (UK). 2015. *Pregnancy and maternity-related discrimination and disadvantage—first findings: Surveys of employers and mothers*. BIS Research Paper No. 235. London: Department for Business, Innovation and Skills and the Equality and Human Rights Commission.
3. Aeberhard-Hodges, Jane. 1996. "Sexual harassment in employment: Recent judicial and arbitral trends." *International Labour Review* 135, no. 5: 499–533.
4. Pillinger, Jane. 2017. *Violence and harassment against women and men in the world of work: Trade union perspectives and action*. Geneva: ILO.
5. Oxfam America. 2015. *Working in fear: Sexual violence against women farmworkers in the United States*. Boston and Washington, DC: Oxfam America.
6. Society for Human Resource Management (US). 2012. *The Workplace impact of domestic and sexual violence and stalking*. Alexandria, VA: Society for Human Resource Management.

Chapter 11

1. International Labour Organization. 2017. *Short-term migrant workers: The case of Ukraine*. Geneva: ILO.
2. UN Women. 2015. *Progress of the world's women 2015–2016: Transforming economies, realizing rights*. New York: United Nations.
3. UN Office on Drugs and Crime. 2014. *Global report on trafficking in persons: 2014*. Vienna: UNODC.
4. International Labour Organization. 2018. "Are we committed to end violence against women migrant workers?" Op-Ed, December 13. https://www.ilo.org/global/about-the-ilo/newsroom/news/WCMS_654545/lang--en/index.htm.
5. Meyer, S. R., W. C. Robinson, C. Branchini, N. Abshir, A. A. Mar, and M. R. Decker. 2019. "Gender Differences in Violence and Other Human Rights Abuses Among Migrant Workers on the Thailand–Myanmar Border." *Violence Against Women* 25, no. 8: 945–67.
6. Seager, Joni. 2018. *The Women's Atlas*. Sydney, NSW: Newsouth Publishing.
7. UN General Assembly. 2000. *Protocol to prevent, suppress and punish trafficking in persons, especially women and children,*

supplementing the United Nations Convention against Transnational Organized Crime. A/55/383. New York: United Nations.

Chapter 12

1. Agarwal, B. and P. Panda. 2007. "Toward freedom from domestic violence: The neglected obvious." *Journal of Human Development* 8, no. 3: 359–88.

2. Panda, Pradeep, Jayoti Gupta, Indika Bulankulame, Nandita Bhatla, Swati Chakraborty, and Nata Duvvury. 2006. *Property ownership & inheritance rights of women for social protection—The South Asia experience: Synthesis report of three studies.* Washington, DC: International Center for Research on Women.

3. UN General Assembly. 2019. *Conflict related sexual violence: Report of the United Nations Secretary-General.* S/2019/280. New York: United Nations.

4. United States Department of State. 2014. *Country reports on human rights practices for 2011.* Volume III, *South and Central Asia, Western Hemisphere.* Washington, DC: US Government Printing Office.

5. Buss, Doris. 2018. "Conflict minerals and sexual violence in Central Africa: Troubling research." *Social Politics: International Studies in Gender, State & Society* 25, no. 4: 545–67.

6. ABColombia, Corporación Sisma Mujer, and the US Office on Colombia. 2013. *Colombia: Women, conflict-related sexual violence and the peace process.* London: ABColombia.

7. Rustad, Siri Aas, Gudrun Østby, and Ragnhild Nordås. 2016. "Artisanal mining, conflict, and sexual violence in Eastern DRC." *Extractive Industries and Society* 3, no. 2: 475–84.

Chapter 13

1. Plan International. 2013. *A girl's right to learn without fear: Working to end gender-based violence at school.* Woking: Plan International.

2. UNESCO, Global Education Monitoring Report Team and United Nations Girls' Education Initiative. 2015. *School-related gender-based violence is preventing the achievement of quality education for all.* Policy Paper 17. https://unesdoc.unesco.org/ark:/48223/pf0000232107.

3. Schneider, S. K., L. O'Donnell, A. Steuve, and R. W. Coulter. 2012. "Cyberbullying, school bullying, and psychological distress: A regional census of high school students." *American Journal of Public Health* 102, no. 1: 171–77.

4. UNESCO. 2017. *School Violence and Bullying: Global Status Report.* Paris: UNESCO.

5. UNESCO. 2017. *School violence and bullying: Global status report.* Paris: UNESCO.

6. UNESCO, Global Education Monitoring Report Team and United Nations Girls' Education Initiative. 2015. *School-related gender-based violence is preventing the achievement of quality education for all.* Policy Paper 17. https://unesdoc.unesco.org/ark:/48223/pf0000232107.

7. FHI 360. 2014. *Empowering Adolescent Girls to Lead through Education (EAGLE) Project: A targeted gender analysis of EAGLE-supported school environments.* Washington, DC: FHI 360.

8. UNICEF. 2011. *Tackling violence in schools: A global perspective—Bridging the gap between standards and practice.* New York: UNICEF

9. ICRW. 2011. *Building support for gender equality among adolescents in school: Findings from Mumbai, India.* New Delhi: ICRW.

10. Parkes, J., and J. Heslop. 2013. *Stop Violence against Girls in School: A cross-country analysis of change in Ghana, Kenya and Mozambique.* London: Institute of Education.

11. Das, M., S. Ghosh, E. Miller, B. O'Conner, and R. Verma. 2012. *Engaging coaches and athletes in fostering gender equity: Findings from the Parivartan Program in Mumbai, India.* New Delhi: ICRW and Futures Without Violence.

Chapter 14

1. True, Jacqui. 2012. *The political economy of violence against women.* New York: Oxford University Press.

2. Australian Women's Health Network. 2014. *The impact on women's health of climatic and economic disaster.* Position Paper. Drysdale, Victoria: Australian Women's Health Network.

3. True, Jacqui. 2012. *The political economy of violence against women.* New York: Oxford University Press.

4. Chamberlain, Gethin. 2017. "Why Climate Change is Creating a New Generation of Child Brides," *The Guardian,* November 26. https://www.theguardian.com/society/2017/nov/26/climate-change-creating-generation-of-child-brides-in-africa. See also the website, https://www.bridesofthesun.com/.

5. Internal Displacement Monitoring Center (IDMC). 2015. *Disaster-related Displacement Risk: Measuring the Risk and Addressing its Drivers.* Geneva: IDMC and Norwegian Refugee Council.

6. Asian-Pacific Resource and Research Centre for Women (ARROW) and the Abdul Momen Khan Memorial Foundation (Khan Foundation). 2015. *Women's sexual & reproductive health and rights (SRHR) and climate change: What is the connection? Scoping Study.* Kuala Lumpur, Malaysia, and Dhaka, Bangladesh: ARROW and the Khan Foundation.

7. The Economist Intelligence Unit. 2014. *The South Asia Women's Resilience Index: Examining the role of women in preparing for and recovering from disasters.* London, New York, Hong Kong, and Geneva: The Economist Intelligence Unit.

Chapter 15

1. International Commission of Jurists. 2018. *Achieving justice for gross human rights violations in Myanmar: A baseline study.* ICJ Global Redress and Accountability Initiative. Geneva: International Commission of Jurists.

2. See UN Secretary-General. 2019. *Conflict-related sexual violence: Report of the UN Secretary-General,* S/2019/280, 29 March 2019.

3. Afghanistan Independent Human Rights Commission (AIHRC). 2018. *Summary of the report on violence against women: The causes, context, and situation of violence against women in Afghanistan.* https://www.refworld.org/docid/5ab132774.html.

4. See ABColombia, *Towards Transformative Change: Women and the Implementation of the Colombian Peace Accord,* Bogota, 2019. Also UN Secretary-General. 2018. Report of the Secretary-General on conflict-related sexual violence, S/2018/250, March 23, 2018.

5. Khuloud Alsaba, and Anuj Kapilashrami. 2016. "Understanding women's experiences of violence and the political economy of gender in conflict: the case of Syria." *Reproductive Health Matters* 24.

6. Llewellyn, Aisyah. 2019. "'Shame and humiliation': Aceh's Islamic law violates human rights." *Al Jazeera,* June 28.

7. Guterres, António. 2019. "Address to the 74th session of the UN General Assembly." September 24. https://www.un.org/sg/en/content/sg/speeches/2019-09-24/address-74th-general-assembly.

8. Monash Gender, Peace and Security Centre. 2020. *Building a Stronger Evidence Base: The Impact of Gender Identities, Norms and Relations on Violent Extremism* (A Case Study of Indonesia, Bangladesh and the Philippines). Bangkok: UN Women.

Chapter 16

1. On, M. L., J. Ayre, K. Webster, and L. Moon. 2016. *Examination of the health outcomes of intimate partner violence against women: State of knowledge paper*. ANROWS Landscapes 03/2016. Sydney, NSW: ANROWS.
2. McTavish, Jill R., Jen C. D. MacGregor, C. Nadine Wathen, and Harriet L. MacMillan. 2016. "Children's exposure to intimate partner violence: an overview." *International Review of Psychiatry* 28, no. 5: 504–18.
3. UNICEF. 2006. *Behind Closed Doors: The Impact of Domestic Violence on Children*. New York: UNICEF and The Body Shop.

Chapter 17

1. World Bank and International Finance Corporation. 2014. *Women, Business and the Law: Removing the Restrictions to Enhance Gender Equality*. Washington DC: World Bank and International Finance Corporation.
2. World Bank. 2018. *Women, Business and the Law*. Washington DC: The World Bank Group.
3. Gorbunova, Yulia. 2019. "Are Russian authorities trolling on domestic violence? Government response to European Court defies belief—and the facts." *Human Rights Watch*, November 20.
4. Global Rights. 2008. *Living with violence: A national report on domestic abuse in Afghanistan*. Washington, DC: Global Rights.
5. Jewkes, Rachel, Julienne Corboz, and Andrew Gibbs. 2019. "Violence against Afghan women by husbands, mothers-in-law and siblings-in-law/siblings: Risk markers and health consequences in an analysis of the baseline of a randomised controlled trial." *PLoS ONE* 14, no. 2: e0211361.

Chapter 18

1. Ormston, Rachel, Ciaran Mullholland, and Lucy Setterfield. 2016. *Caledonian system evaluation: Analysis of a programme for tackling domestic abuse in Scotland*. Social Research Series. Edinburgh: The Scottish Government.
2. True, Jacqui. 2017. "Conflict in Asia and the role of gender-based violence." In *Essays on the state of conflict and violence in Asia*, ed. Sana Jaffrey and Dan Slater. San Francisco, CA: The Asia Foundation.
3. Paul, Stella. 2014. "Lack of accountability fuels gender-based violence in India." *IPS News*, September 30.

4. Fulu, Emma, Xian Warner, Stephanie Miedema, Rachel Jewkes, Tim Roselli, and James Lang. 2013. *Why do some men use violence against women and how can we prevent it? Quantitative findings from the United Nations multi-country study on men and violence in Asia and the Pacific.* Bangkok: United Nations.
5. Wolfe, D., C. Crooks, P. Jaffe, D. Chiodo, R. Hughes, W. Ellis, L. Stitt, and A. Donner. 2009. "A schoolbased program to prevent adolescent dating violence: A cluster randomised trial." *Archives of Pediatric and Adolescent Medicine* 163, no. 8: 692–9.
6. Tamagno, Carla, and Cheri Varnadoe. 2018. *Public and private sectors' strategies to prevent gender-based violence, reduce costs and develop capacity in APEC economies.* APEC Policy Partnership on Women and the Economy. Singapore: APEC.
7. Mastonshoeva, Subhiya, Shahribonu Shonasimova, Dilorom Abdulhaeva, Henri Myrttinen, Rachel Jewkes, and Nwabisa Shai. 2018. *Working with families to prevent violence against women and girls in Tajikistan.* Evidence Brief. https://www.whatworks.co.za/resources/evidence-reviews/item/462-working-with-families-to-prevent-violence-against-women-and-girls-in-tajikistan.
8. Addo-Lartey, Adolphina, Deda Ogum Alangea, Esnat Chirwa, Dorcas Coker-Appiah, Rachel Jewkes, Richard M. K. Adanu, and Yandisa Sikweyiya. 2019. *Impact assessment: Rural response system intervention to prevent violence against women and girls in four districts, Central Region of Ghana.* Evidence Brief. https://www.whatworks.co.za/resources/policy-briefs/item/675-impact-assessment-rural-response-system-intervention-to-prevent-violence-against-women-and-girls-in-four-districts-central-region-of-ghana.

Chapter 19
1. Boonzaier, Floretta. 2008. "'If the man says you must sit, then you must sit': The relational construction of woman abuse—Gender, subjectivity and violence." *Feminism & Psychology* 18, no. 2: 183–206.
2. American Civil Liberties Union. 2006. *Domestic Violence and Homelessness.* New York: ACLU. https://www.aclu.org/sites/default/files/pdfs/dvhomelessness032106.pdf.
3. Australia's National Research Organisation for Women's Safety (ANROWS). 2018. *Violence against women: Accurate use of key statistics.* ANROWS Insights 05/2018. Sydney, NSW: ANROWS.

4. UN Women. 2017. "UN Women and ESCWA launch project to estimate the cost of violence against women in the Arab Region." *UN Women News*, October 10.

5. Australia's National Research Organisation for Women's Safety (ANROWS). 2018. *Violence against women: Accurate use of key statistics*. ANROWS Insights 05/2018. Sydney, NSW: ANROWS.

6. ISSER, Ipsos MORI, International Centre for Research on Women and NUI Galway. 2019. *Economic and Social Costs of Violence Against Women and Girls: Ghana*. Summary Report. Galway: NUI Galway. https://www.ipsos.com/sites/default/files/ct/publication/documents/2019-07/economic-social-costs-violence-women-girls-ghana-2019.pdf.

7. What Works to Prevent Violence against Women and Girls Programme (UK Department for International Development). 2019. *A family-centred intervention to prevent Violence against Women and Girls in migrant communities of Baglung District, Nepal*. Evidence Brief. https://www.whatworks.co.za/resources/policy-briefs/item/564-a-family-centred-intervention-to-prevent-violence-against-women-and-girls-in-migrant-communities-of-baglung-district-nepal.

8. Howard, Marilyn, and Amy Skipp. 2015. *Unequal, trapped & controlled: Women's experience of financial abuse and potential implications for universal credit*. London: Trades Union Congress.

Chapter 20

1. Moosa, Zohra. 2015. *A theory of change for tackling violence against women and girls*. Chard, UK: ActionAid UK.

2. Heise, L. 1998. "Violence against women, an integrated, ecological framework." *Violence Against Women* 4, no. 4: 262–90.

3. Manikam, Shamini. 2012. *A literature review on domestic violence campaigns and the use of technology as a prevention strategy*. Final Report, Queensland University of Technology. https://research.qut.edu.au/servicesocialmarketing/wp-content/uploads/sites/28/2017/02/Literature-Review-on-Domestic-Violence-Technology-and-Theory.pdf.

4. Roguski, Michael. 2015. *"It's Not Ok" campaign community evaluation project*. New Zealand: Ministry of Social Development.

5. Victorian Law Reform Commission. 2001. *Sexual offences: Law and procedure*. Discussion Paper. Melbourne, Victoria: Victorian Law Reform Commission.

6. Bacman, Keren. 2016. "The 'Ni Una Menos' effect: More women in Buenos Aires are denouncing violence." *TheBubble*, August 31.
7. GirlUp. 2020. *SchoolCycle Malawi* (web page). https://www.girlup.org/schoolcycle/malawi/.
8. National Statistical Office (NSO) and ICF. 2017. *Malawi demographic and health survey 2015–16.* Zomba, Malawi, and Rockville, MD: NSO and ICF.
9. Hall, Rebecca Jane. 2015. "Feminist strategies to end violence against women." In *The Oxford handbook of transnational feminist movements*, ed. Rawwida Baksh and Wendy Harcourt. New York: Oxford University Press, 394–415.
10. Wellington, Shahni, and Jack Latimore. 2019. "Chair of indigenous family violence peak body says funding cuts opposite of recommendations in recent report." *NITV-SBS*, December 6. https://www.sbs.com.au/nitv/article/2019/12/06/chair-indigenous-family-violence-peak-body-says-funding-cuts-opposite.
11. Native Women's Association Canada. 2015. *Fact sheet: Missing and murdered aboriginal women and girls.* Ottawa, ON: Native Women's Association Canada.
12. Australian Institute of Health and Welfare. 2018. *Family, domestic and sexual violence in Australia.* Canberra: Australian Institute of Health and Welfare.

SUGGESTED SOURCES

Chapter 1

Šimonović, Dubravka. 2019. "Ending Violence against Women and Girls: Progress and Remaining Challenges." *UN Chronicle*, November 25.

True, Jacqui. 2012. *The Political Economy of Violence against Women.* New York: Oxford University Press.

UN Convention on the Elimination of All Forms of Discrimination against Women (CEDAW). 1992. *CEDAW General Recommendation No. 19: Violence against Women.* 11th Session.

UN Department of Economic and Social Affairs (UN DESA), Statistics Division. 2015. *The World's Women 2015: Trends and Statistics.* New York: United Nations.

UN General Assembly. 1993. *Declaration on the Elimination of Violence against Women.* UN Doc. A/RES/48/104, December 20.

Websites/Web Pages

Centre for Sexualities, AIDS and Gender (University of Pretoria). *"Hidden Traumas"—When Men Are Victims of Gender-Based and Sexual Violence.* https://www.justgender.org/hidden-traumas-when-men-are-victims-of-gender-based-and-sexual-violence/.

UN Office of the High Commissioner for Human Rights, Committee on the Elimination of Discrimination against Women. https://www.ohchr.org/en/hrbodies/cedaw/pages/cedawindex.aspx.

Chapter 2

Brownmiller, Susan. 1975. *Against Our Will: Men, Women and Rape.* New York: Simon & Schuster.

Gerhardt, Elizabeth. 2014. *The Cross and Gendercide: A Theological Response to Global Violence Against Women and Girls*. Downers Grove, IL: IVP Academics.

Keck, Margaret E., and Kathryn Sikkink. "Transnational Networks on Violence against Women." In *Activists Beyond Borders: Advocacy Networks in International Politics*. Ithaca, NY: Cornell University Press.

Reinelt, Claire. 1995. "Moving onto the Terrain of the State: The Battered Women's Movement and the Politics of Engagement." In *Feminist Organizations: Harvest of the New Women's Movement*, edited by Myra Marx Ferree and Patricia Yancey Martin. Philadelphia: Temple University Press.

Schechter, Susan. 1982. *Women and Male Violence: The Visions and Struggles of the Battered Women's Movement*. Cambridge, MA: South End Press.

Valk, Anne. 2017. "Remembering Together: Take Back the Night and the Public Memory of Feminism." In *U.S. Women's History: Untangling the Threads of Sisterhood*, edited by Leslie Brown, Jacqueline Castledine, and Anne Valk. New Brunswick, NJ: Rutgers University Press.

Websites

Reclaim the Night (UK): http://www.reclaimthenight.co.uk/.

Take Back the Night (US): https://takebackthenight.org/.

UN Women, *Women of the World, Unite!*: https://interactive.unwomen.org/multimedia/timeline/womenunite/en/index.html#/.

Chapter 3

Heise, Lori L., and Andreas Kotsadam. 2015. "Cross-National and Multilevel Correlates of Partner Violence: An Analysis of Data from Population-Based Surveys." *Lancet Global Health* 3, no. 6: 332–40.

Kandala, Ngianga-Bakwin Kandala, Martinsixtus C. Ezejimofor, Olalekan A. Uthman, and Paul Komba. 2017. "Secular Trends in the Prevalence of Female Genital Mutilation/Cutting among Girls: A Systematic Analysis." *BMJ Global Health* 3, no. 5. https://gh.bmj.com/content/3/5/e000549.

Levinson, D. 1989. *Family Violence in Cross-Cultural Perspective*. Newbury Park, CA: Sage.

Tavares, Paula, and Quentin Wodon. 2018. *Global and Regional Trends in Women's Legal Protection against Domestic Violence and Sexual*

Harassment. Ending Violence against Women Notes Series. Washington, DC: The World Bank.

Thomson Reuters Foundation. 2018. "The World's Most Dangerous Countries for Women." Annual Poll. https://poll2018.trust.org.

World Health Organization. 2005. *WHO Multi-Country Study on Women's Health and Domestic Violence against Women: Initial Results on Prevalence, Health Outcomes and Women's Responses*. Summary Report. Geneva: World Health Organization.

Websites

UN Women, *Ending Violence against Women and Girls with Disabilities*: https://www2.unwomen.org/-/media/field%20office%20untf/publications/2018/untf%202pagerdisability%20and%20vaw%20finalcompressed.pdf?la=en&vs=953.

VAWnet database: https://vawnet.org/.

World Bank, *Gender Equality*: http://datatopics.worldbank.org/sdgatlas/archive/2017/SDG-05-gender-equality.html.

Chapter 4

International Parliamentary Union. 2019. *Violence against Women in Parliament*. https://www.ipu.org/our-impact/gender-equality/womens-rights/combatting-violence-against-women/violence-against-women-in-parliament.

Organisation for Economic Co-operation and Development. 2019. *Social Institutions and Gender Index: 2019 Results*. https://www.genderindex.org/ranking/.

Uggen, Christopher, and Amy Blackstone. 2004. "Sexual Harassment as a Gendered Expression of Power." *American Sociological Review* 69, no. 1: 64–92.

UN Office for the High Commissioner of Human Rights (OHCHR). 2015. *Women Human Rights Defenders*. Information Series on Sexual and Reproductive Health and Rights. https://www.ohchr.org/Documents/Issues/Women/WRGS/SexualHealth/INFO_WHRD_WEB.pdf.

UN Statistics Division. 2018. *Minimum Set of Gender Indicators*. https://genderstats.un.org/#/home.

Websites

The Equality Institute: http://www.equalityinstitute.org/.

OECD, *Violence against Women Indicator*: https://data.oecd.org/inequality/violence-against-women.htm.

UN Women, *Two Sides of the Same Coin: Gender Inequality and Violence against Women*: https://www.unwomen.org/en/news/stories/2017/10/speech-ed-phumzile-five-days-of-violence-prevention-conference.

Chapter 5

Baaz, Maria Ericksson, and Maria Stern. 2013. *Sexual Violence as a Weapon of War? Perceptions, Prescriptions, Problems in the Congo and Beyond*. London: Zed Books.

Cohen, Dara Kay, and Ragnild Nordås. 2014. "Sexual Violence in Armed Conflict: Introducing the SVAC Dataset, 1989–2009." *Journal of Peace Research* 51, no. 3: 418–28.

Development Alternatives with Women for a New Era (DAWN). 2019. *The Political Economy of Gender and Conflict*. London: Zed Books.

Henry, Nicola. 2011. *War and Rape: Law, Memory and Justice*. London: Routledge.

Swaine, Aisling. 2017. *Conflict-Related Violence against Women: Transforming Transition*. New York: Cambridge University Press.

Websites

Crisis Group, *Gender, Peace and Security*: https://www.crisisgroup.org/gender-peace-and-security.

Nuremberg Academy, *Sexual Crimes in Conflict Database*: https://www.nurembergacademy.org/resources/sexual-crimes-in-conflict-database/database/.

OHCHR, *Women's Human Rights and Gender-Related Concerns in Situations of Conflict and Instability*: https://www.ohchr.org/EN/Issues/Women/WRGS/Pages/PeaceAndSecurity.aspx.

Chapter 6

Bjarnegård, Elin, Karen Brounéus, and Erik Melander. 2017. "Beliefs about Male Superiority Help Explain Why More Gender-equal Societies Are More Peaceful." *Political Violence at a Glance*, November 8.

Flood, Michael. 2018. *Engaging Men and Boys in Violence Prevention*. New York: Palgrave.

Flood, Michael. 2018. "Men Building Gender Equality: A Guide to XY's Content." *XY Online*, April 14. https://xyonline.net/content/men-building-gender-equality-guide-xys-content.

Salter, Michael. 2016. "Real Men Do Hit Women: The Violence at the Heart of Masculinity." *Meanjin* 75, no. 1: 97–104.

TEDx Talks. 2013. "Violence against Women—It's a Men's Issue: Jackson Katz at TEDxFiDiWomen." Video, February 11. https://www.youtube.com/watch?v=KTvSfeCRxe8.

Websites

American Psychological Association, *Harmful Masculinity and Violence*: https://www.apa.org/pi/about/newsletter/2018/09/harmful-masculinity.

BroadAgenda, *Violence against Women: A Crisis of Masculinity? Part 1*: http://www.broadagenda.com.au/home/beyond-the-male-vs-female-divide-a-crisis-of-masculinity-pt-1/.

Chapter 7

Farage, Miranda A., Kenneth W. Miller, Ghebre E. Tzeghai, Charles E. Azuka, Jack D. Sobel, and William J. Ledger. 2015. "Female Genital Cutting: Confronting Cultural Challenges and Health Complications across the Lifespan." *Women's Health* 11, no. 1: 79–94.

Karen Human Rights Group. 2018. *Suffering in Silence? Sexual Violence against Women in Southeast Myanmar*. News Bulletin, December. Myanmar: Karen Human Rights Group.

Merry, Sally Engle. 2008. *Gender Violence: A Cultural Perspective*. New York: John Wiley & Sons.

Okin, Susan Moller. 1999. *Is Multiculturalism Bad for Women?* Princeton, NJ: Princeton University Press.

Oxfam GB. 2018. *Breaking a Culture of Silence: Social Norms That Perpetuate Violence against Women and Girls in Nigeria*. Research Report, February 28. Nigeria: Oxfam Novib.

Rao, Arati. 1995. "The Politics of Gender and Culture in International Human Rights Discourse." In *Women's Rights, Human Rights: International Feminist Perspectives*, edited by Julie Peters and Andrea Wolper. New York: Routledge.

Websites

The Conversation, *Gender, Culture and Class Collude in Violence against Women*: https://theconversation.com/gender-culture-and-class-collude-in-violence-against-women-22957.

Multicultural Centre for Women's Health, *Intersectionality Matters: A Guide to Engaging Immigrant and Refugee Communities to Prevent Violence against Women*: https://www.mcwh.com.au/downloads/Intersectionality-Matters-Guide-2017.pdf.

Chapter 8

Baluta, O. 2015. "Representing and Consuming Women: Paradoxes in Media Covering Violence against Women." *Journal of Media Research* 8, no. 2: 52–67.

Bogen, Katherine W., Kaitlyn K. Bleiweiss, Nykia R. Leach, and Lindsay M. Orchowski. 2019. "#MeToo: Disclosure and Response to Sexual Victimization on Twitter." *Journal of Interpersonal Violence*: 1–32. doi:10.1177/0886260519851211.

Easteal, Patricia, Kate Holland, and Keziah Judd. 2015. "Enduring Themes and Silences in Media Portrayals of Violence against Women." *Women's Studies International Forum* 48: 103–13.

Henry, Nicola, and Asher Flynn. 2019. "Image-Based Sexual Abuse: Online Distribution Channels and Illicit Communities of Support." *Violence Against Women* 25, no. 16: 1932–55.

Macharia, Sarah. 2015. *Who Makes the News?* Global Media and Monitoring Project 2015. London/Toronto: World Association for Christian Communication.

Women's Media Center. 2015. *Writing Rape: How the U.S. Media Cover Campus Rape and Sexual Assault.* New York and Washington, DC: Women's Media Center.

Websites

MeToo movement: https://metoomvmt.org/.

TIME'S UP movement: https://timesupnow.org/.

UNESCO, *Violence against Women in the Media*: https://en.unesco.org/themes/violence-against-women-and-girls-media.

Chapter 9

Amaral, S., S. Bandyopadhyay, and R. Sensarma. 2015. *Public Work Programs and Gender-based Violence: The Case of NREGA in India.* Birmingham University, Department of Economics Discussion Paper 15–09.

KPMG. 2017. *Too Costly to Ignore: The Economic Impact of Gender-Based Violence in South Africa.* Johannesburg, South Africa: KPMG Human and Social Services.

UN Women. 2013. *Study on Ways and Methods to Eliminate Sexual Harassment in Egypt.* Cairo: UN Women.

World Bank. 2014. *Voice and Agency: Empowering Women and Girls for Shared Prosperity.* Washington, DC: World Bank Group.

World Bank. 2019. *Women, Business and the Law: A Decade of Reform.* Washington, DC: World Bank Group.

Websites

UN Women, *Women and Poverty*: https://beijing20.unwomen.org/en/
in-focus/poverty.

World Bank, *To End Poverty, Eliminate Gender-Based Violence*: https://
www.youtube.com/watch?v=K0YXt_dfnxY.

Chapter 10

International Labour Organization. 2018. *Ending Violence and Harassment
Against Women and Men in the World of Work*. Geneva: ILO.

MacKinnon, Catharine. 1979. *Sexual Harassment of Working Women: A
Case of Sex Discrimination*. New Haven, CT: Yale University Press.

Rider-Milkovich, Holly, and Elizabeth Bille. 2019. "Let's Get to
Work: Empowering Employees to Take Action on Domestic
Violence." *Ms.*, October 24.

Trade Union Congress. 2015. *Unequal, Trapped and Controlled: Women's
Experience of Financial Abuse and Potential Implications for Universal
Credit*. London: Trades Union Congress.

UN Women. 2019. *Handbook: Addressing Violence and Harassment against
Women in the World of Work*. New York: UN Women.

Websites

International Labour Organization, *ILO Convention on Violence and
Harassment: Five Key Questions*: https://www.ilo.org/global/
about-the-ilo/newsroom/news/WCMS_711891/lang--en/index.
htm.

openDemocracy, *The Crisis of Workplace Violence against Women*: https://
www.opendemocracy.net/en/beyond-trafficking-and-slavery/
crisis-of-workplace-violence-against-women/.

openDemocracy, *Precarious Work Makes Women More Vulnerable to
Gender-Based Violence*: https://www.opendemocracy.net/en/
oureconomy/precarious-work-makes-women-more-vulnerable-
gender-based-violence/.

Chapter 11

Fernandez, Manny. 2018. "They Were Stopped at the Texas
Border: Their Nightmare Had Only Just Begun." *New York Times*,
November 12.

Meyer, S. R., W. C. Robinson, C. Branchini, N. Abshir, A. A. Mar, and M.
R. Decker. 2019. "Gender Differences in Violence and Other Human
Rights Abuses among Migrant Workers on the Thailand–Myanmar
Border." *Violence Against Women* 25, no. 8: 945–67.

Servin, A., A. Rocha-Jimenez, R. Munoz, and K. Brouwer. 2018. "Labor Exploitation and Sexual Violence in Latin America: The Experience of Central American Migrant Women." *European Journal of Public Health* 28, supp. 1: 5.1–O1.

UN General Assembly. 2018. *Trafficking in Women and Girls: Report of the Secretary-General.* Seventy-Third Session, A/73/263. New York: United Nations.

UN General Assembly. 2019. *Violence against Women Migrant Workers: Report of the Secretary-General.* Seventy-Fourth Session, A/74/235. New York: United Nations.

Websites

Human Rights Watch, 2014, *"I Already Bought You"*: https://www.hrw.org/report/2014/10/22/i-already-bought-you/abuse-and-exploitation-female-migrant-domestic-workers-united.

Human Rights Watch, 2016, *"I Was Sold"*: https://www.hrw.org/report/2016/07/13/i-was-sold/abuse-and-exploitation-migrant-domestic-workers-oman.

Polaris, *Human Trafficking: The Facts*: https://polarisproject.org/human-trafficking/facts.

Chapter 12

Grabe S., R. G. Grose, and A. Dutt. 2015. "Women's Land Ownership and Relationship Power: A Mixed Methods Approach to Understanding Structural Inequities and Violence against Women." *Psychology of Women Quarterly* 39, no 1: 7–19.

Hilliard, Starr, Elizabeth Bukusi, Shelly Grabe, Tiffany Lu, Abigail M. Hatcher, Zachary Kwena, Esther Mwaura-Muiru, and Shari L. Dworkin. 2016. "Perceived Impact of a Land and Property Rights Program on Violence against Women in Rural Kenya: A Qualitative Investigation." *Violence Against Women* 22, no. 14: 1682–1703.

Lahiri-Dutt, K. 2008. "Digging to Survive: Women's Livelihoods in South Asia's Small Mines and Quarries." *South Asian Survey* 15, no. 2: 217–44.

Song, Yueping, and Xiao-Yuan Dong. 2017. "Domestic Violence and Women's Land Rights in Rural China: Findings from a National Survey in 2010." *Journal of Development Studies* 53, no. 9: 1471–85.

Vyas, Seema, Henrica A. F. M. Jansen, Lori Heise, and Jessie Mbwambo. 2015. "Exploring the Association between Women's Access to Economic Resources and Intimate Partner Violence in

Dar es Salaam and Mbeya, Tanzania." *Social Science & Medicine* 146: 307–15.

World Bank. 2018. *Good Practice Note: Addressing Gender-Based Violence in Investment Project Financing Involving Major Civil Works.* Washington, DC: World Bank Group.

Websites

International Institute for Sustainable Development, *Connecting the Dots: Natural Resources, Women and Peace*: https://www.iisd.org/blog/connecting-dots-natural-resources-women-and-peace.

UN Women Asia-Pacific, *Women's Land & Property Rights*: https://asiapacific.unwomen.org/en/focus-areas/women-poverty-economics/women-s-land-property-rights.

Chapter 13

Achyut, P., N. Bhatla, H. Verma, Singh G. Uttamacharya, S. Bhattacharya, and R. Verma. 2016. *Towards Gender Equality: The GEMS Journey thus Far.* New Delhi: International Center for Research on Women.

Association of American Universities (AAU). 2019. *Report on the AAU campus Climate Survey on Sexual Assault and Misconduct.* September 21. https://www.aau.edu/key-issues/campus-climate-and-safety/aau-campus-climate-survey-2019.

Australian Human Rights Commission. 2017. *Change the Course: National Report on Sexual Assault and Sexual Harassment at Australian Universities.* August. https://www.humanrights.gov.au/our-work/sex-discrimination/publications/change-course-national-report-sexual-assault-and-sexual.

Plan International. 2013. *A Girl's Right to Learn without Fear: Working to End Gender-Based Violence at School.* Woking: Plan International.

UNESCO and UN Women. 2016. *Global Guidance: School-Related Gender-Based Violence.* Paris: UNESCO.

Websites

Asian Development Blog, *How to Integrate Violence against Women Prevention, Response in Education*: https://blogs.adb.org/blog/how-integrate-violence-against-women-prevention-response-education.

Global Initiative to End All Corporal Punishment, *Corporal Punishment in Schools*: https://endcorporalpunishment.org/schools/.

Tomorrow Man Australia: https://www.tomorrowman.com.au/.

Chapter 14

Alston, M. 2014. "Gender Mainstreaming and Climate Change." *Women's Studies International Forum* 47: 287–94.

Human Rights Watch. 2015. *Marry Before Your House Is Swept Away*. New York: Human Rights Watch.

International Fund for Agricultural Development. 2014. *The Gender Advantage: Women on the Front Line of Climate Change*. Rome: IFAD.

Jaggernath, Jyoti. 2014. "Women, Climate Change and Environmentally-Induced Conflicts in Africa." *Agenda* 28, no. 3: 90–101.

Tanyag, M., and J. True. 2019. *Gender Responsive Alternatives to Climate Change: A Global Research Report*. Melbourne: Monash Gender, Peace and Security Centre with ActionAid International. https://actionaid.org.au/wp-content/uploads/2019/11/Monash-GRACC-Report-Global-.pdf.

Websites

ActionAid, *The South Asia Women's Resilience Index*: https://actionaid.org.au/resources/the-south-asia-womens-resilience-index/.

International Union for Conservation of Nature, *Environment Gender Index*: https://genderandenvironment.org/resource/the-environment-gender-index/.

UN Environment, *Women, Natural Resources and Peace*: https://www.unenvironment.org/explore-topics/disasters-conflicts/what-we-do/recovery/women-natural-resources-and-peace.

Chapter 15

Bjarnegård, Elin, Karen Brounéus, and Erik Melander. 2017. "Honor and Political Violence: Micro-level Findings from a Survey in Thailand." *Journal of Peace Research* 54, no. 6: 748–61.

Castillo-Díaz, Pablo, and Nahla Valji. 2019. "Symbiosis of Misogyny and Violent Extremism: New Understandings and Policy Implications." *Journal of International Affairs* 72, no. 2: 37–56.

Davies, Sara E., and Jacqui True. 2019. *The Oxford Handbook on Women, Peace and Security*. New York: Oxford University Press.

Hudson, Valerie M., Bonnie Ballif-Spanvill, Mary Caprioli, and Chad F. Emmett. 2012. *Sex and World Peace*. New York: Colombia University Press.

Johnson, Melissa, and Jacqui True. 2019. "Misogyny and Violent Extremism: Implications for Preventing Violent Extremism."

Research Brief. Monash Gender, Peace and Security Centre.
    https://arabstates.unwomen.org/en/digital-library/publications/
    2019/10/wps-policy-brief.
Smith, Joan. 2019. *Home Grown: How Domestic Violence Turns Men into
    Terrorists*. London: Riverrun.

Websites

Foreign Affairs, *Violence Against Women and International
    Security*: https://www.foreignaffairs.com/articles/world/2017-11-
    28/violence-against-women-and-international-security.
Monash University, *Monash Gender, Peace and Security Centre*: https://
    www.monash.edu/arts/gender-peace-security.
UN Women, *Women, Peace and Security*: https://unwomen.org.au/our-
    work/focus-areas/women-peace-and-security/.

Chapter 16

Bourget, Dominique, Jennifer Grace, and Laurie Whitehurst. 2007. "A
    Review of Maternal and Paternal Filicide." *Journal of the American
    Academy of Psychiatry and the Law* 35, no. 1: 74–82.
McTavish, Jill R., Jen C. D. MacGregor, C. Nadine Wathen, and Harriet
    L. MacMillan. 2016. "Children's Exposure to Intimate Partner
    Violence: An Overview." *International Review of Psychiatry* 28, no.
    5: 504–18.
Mogos, Mulubrhan F., Winta N. Araya, Saba W. Masho, Jason L. Salemi,
    Carol Shieh, and Hamisu M. Salihu. 2016. "The Feto-Maternal
    Health Cost of Intimate Partner Violence among Delivery-Related
    Discharges in the United States, 2002–2009." *Journal of Interpersonal
    Violence* 31, no. 3: 444–64.
Price-Robertson, R., D. Higgins, and S. Vassallo. 2013. "Multi-type
    Maltreatment and Polyvictimisation: A Comparison of Two
    Research Frameworks." *Family Matters* 93: 84–98.
Scutella, R., A. Chigavazira, E. Killackey, N. Herault, G. Johnson, J.
    Moschion, and M. Wooden. 2014. *Journeys Home Research Report
    No. 4: Findings from Waves 1 to 4 (Special Topics)*. Research report.
    Melbourne: Melbourne Institute of Applied Economic and Social
    Research.
World Health Organization (WHO). 2013 . *Global and Regional Estimates
    of Violence against Women: Prevalence and Health Effects of Intimate
    Partner Violence and Non-partner Sexual Violence*. Geneva: WHO.

Websites

ANROWS, *Examination of the Health Outcomes of Intimate Partner Violence against Women: State of Knowledge Paper*: https://www.anrows.org.au/publication/examination-of-the-health-outcomes-of-intimate-partner-violence-against-women-state-of-knowledge-paper/.

Australian Institute of Family Studies, *Children's Exposure to Domestic and Family Violence*: https://aifs.gov.au/cfca/publications/childrens-exposure-domestic-and-family-violence/export.

Guttmacher Institute, *Understanding Intimate Partner Violence as a Sexual and Reproductive Health and Rights Issue in the United States*: https://www.guttmacher.org/gpr/2016/07/understanding-intimate-partner-violence-sexual-and-reproductive-health-and-rights-issue.

Chapter 17

Human Rights Watch. 2017. *"Your Destiny Is to Stay with Him": State Response to Domestic Violence in Algeria*. New York: Human Rights Watch.

Human Rights Watch. 2018. "Russia: Unaddressed Domestic Violence Puts Women at Risk." News Release, October 25. https://www.hrw.org/news/2018/10/25/russia-unaddressed-domestic-violence-puts-women-risk.

Manjoo, Rashida. 2012. "The Continuum of Violence against Women and the Challenges of Effective Redress." *International Human Rights Law Review* 1, no. 1: 1–29.

Tavares, Paula, and Quentin Wodon. 2018. *Global and Regional Trends in Women's Legal Protection against Domestic Violence and Sexual Harassment*. Ending Violence against Women Notes Series. Washington, DC: World Bank Group.

UN Economic and Social Council. 2006. *Integration of the Human Rights of Women and the Gender Perspective: Violence against Women—The Due Diligence Standard as a Tool for the Elimination of Violence against Women*. Commission on Human Rights, Sixty-Second Session, January 20, Provisional agenda item 12 (a), E/CN.4/2006/61. Geneva: United Nations.

UN Human Rights Council. 2017. *Report of the Special Rapporteur on Violence against Women, Its Causes and Consequences*. Thirty-Fifth Session, A/HRC/35/30. Geneva: United Nations.

Websites

Equality Now, *Russia Is Failing in Its Obligations to Protect Women from Domestic and Sexual Violence*: https://www.equalitynow.org/russia_domestic_and_sexual_violence.

LSE Centre for Women, Peace and Security, *Tackling Violence against Women: A–Z of Cases*: https://blogs.lse.ac.uk/vaw/landmark-cases/a-z-of-cases/.

US Attorney's Office, Western Distinct of Tennessee, *Federal Domestic Violence Laws*: https://www.justice.gov/usao-wdtn/victim-witness-program/federal-domestic-violence-laws.

Chapter 18

Carrington, Kerry, Máximo Sozzo, María Victoria Puyol, Marcela Parada Gamboa, Natacha Guala, and Diego Zysman. 2019. *The Role of Women's Police Stations in Responding to and Preventing Gender Violence, Buenos Aires, Argentina: Stage 1 Report ARC Project*. Brisbane: Queensland University of Technology.

Goodmark, Leigh. 2018. *Decriminalizing Domestic Violence: A Balanced Policy Approach to Intimate Partner Violence*. Oakland: University of California Press.

Perova, Elizaveta, and Sarah Anne Reynolds. 2017. "Women's Police Stations and Intimate Partner Violence: Evidence from Brazil." *Social Science & Medicine* 174: 188–96.

UN Office on Drugs and Crime. 2014. *Handbook on Effective Prosecution Responses to Violence against Women and Girls*. Criminal Justice Handbook Series. Vienna: UNODC.

UN Women. 2011. *Progress of the World's Women 2011–2012: In Pursuit of Justice*. New York: United Nations.

World Health Organization. 2009. *Changing Cultural and Social Norms Supportive of Violent Behavior*. Series of Briefings on Violence Prevention: The Evidence. Geneva: WHO.

Websites

What Works to Prevent Violence, *Impact Assessment: Rural Response System Intervention to Prevent Violence against Women and Girls in Four Districts, Central Region of Ghana*: https://www.whatworks.co.za/documents/publications/364-prevent-violence-against-women-and-girls-in-four-districts-ghana4/file.

What Works to Prevent Violence, *Working with Families to Prevent Violence against Women and Girls in Tajikistan*: https://www.whatworks.co.za/resources/evidence-reviews/item/462-working-with-families-to-prevent-violence-against-women-and-girls-in-tajikistan.

Chapter 19

Asia-Pacific Economic Cooperation. 2017. *Public and Private Sectors' Strategies to Prevent Gender-based Violence, Reduce Costs and Develop Capacity in APEC Economies*. APEC Policy Partnership on Women and the Economy, December 2017.

Duvvury, Nata, Patricia Carney, and Nguyen Huu Minh. 2012. *Estimating the Costs of Domestic Violence against Women in Viet Nam*. Hanoi: UN Women Viet Nam Country Office.

Fahmy, E., E. Williamson, and C. Pantazis. 2016. *Evidence and Policy Review: Domestic Violence and Poverty*. London: Joseph Rowntree Foundation.

Gibbs, Andrew, and Kate Bishop. 2019. *Preventing Violence against Women and Girls: Combined Economic Empowerment and Gender-Transformative Interventions*. Evidence Review, What Works to Prevent Violence: A Global Programme, September.

Kaukinen, C. E., and R. A. Powers. 2015. "The Role of Economic Factors on Women's Risk for Intimate Partner Violence: A Cross-National Comparison of Canada and the United States." *Violence Against Women* 21, no. 2: 229–48.

Schneider, D., K. Harknett, and S. McLanahan. 2016. "Intimate Partner Violence in the Great Recession." *Demography* 53, no. 2: 471–505.

Websites

American Civil Liberties Union, *Domestic Violence and Homelessness*: https://www.aclu.org/other/domestic-violence-and-homelessness.

International Women's Development Agency, *Economic Empowerment, Gender Norms and Violence Against Women*: https://iwda.org.au/economic-empowerment-gender-norms-and-violence-against-women/.

openDemocracy, *Austerity and Domestic Violence: Mapping the Damage*: https://www.opendemocracy.net/en/5050/austerity-and-domestic-violence-mapping-damage/.

Chapter 20

Hall, Rebecca Jane. 2015. "Feminist Strategies to End Violence against Women." In *The Oxford Handbook of Transnational Feminist Movements*, edited by Rawwida Baksh and Wendy Harcourt, 394–416. Oxford: Oxford University Press.

Politi, Daniel, and Ernesto Londoño. 2018. "They Lost Argentina's Abortion Vote, but Advocates Started a Movement." *New York Times*, August 9.

Salter, Michael. 2016. "'Real Men Don't Hit Women': Constructing
    Masculinity in the Prevention of Violence against Women."
    Australian and New Zealand Journal of Criminology 49, no. 4: 463–79.
Weldon, S. Laurel and Mala Htun. 2013. "Feminist Mobilisation and
    Progressive Policy Change: Why Governments Take Action to
    Combat Violence against Women." *Gender & Development* 21, no.
    2: 231–47.
World Health Organization. 2009. *Changing Cultural and Social Norms
    Supportive of Violent Behavior*. Series of Briefings on Violence
    Prevention: The Evidence. Geneva: WHO.

Websites
Australian Government Productivity Commission, *Overcoming
    Indigenous Disadvantage*: https://www.pc.gov.au/research/
    ongoing/overcoming-indigenous-disadvantage.
It's Not Okay NZ: http://www.areyouok.org.nz/.
Ni Una Menos (Spanish): http://niunamenos.org.ar/

INDEX

For the benefit of digital users, indexed terms that span two pages (e.g., 52–53) may, on occasion, appear on only one of those pages.